THE *Complete* HEDGEHOG

D0259393

THE
Complete
HEDGEHOG

LES STOCKER

Foreword by John Craven

Drawings by Ian Mackay

Chatto & Windus/London

Published in 1987
by Chatto & Windus Ltd
30 Bedford Square
London WC1B 3RP

All rights reserved. No part of this
publication may be reproduced, stored in a
retrieval system, or transmitted in any form,
or by any means, electronic, mechanical,
photocopying, recording or otherwise, without
the prior permission of the publisher.

British Library Cataloguing in Publication Data

Stocker, Les
  The complete hedgehog.
  1. Hedgehogs
  I. Title
  599.3'3   QL737.I53
  ISBN 0-7011-3272-8

Copyright © Les Stocker 1987

Photoset in Linotron Baskerville
by Rowland Phototypesetting Ltd
Bury St Edmunds, Suffolk
Printed in Great Britain by
Redwood Burn Ltd
Trowbridge, Wiltshire

The poem 'In Defence of Hedgehogs'
© Pam Ayres, p. 99, is reproduced by
permission of Pam Ayres.
Drawings by Ian Mackay.
Map by John Flower.
Photographs, except where otherwise
credited, are by Les Stocker.
The logo of the Keep Britain Tidy Group
p. 39 is reproduced with their kind
permission. 'Mrs Tiggy-winkle' p. 35 is
from *The Tale of Mrs Tiggy-winkle*
by Beatrix Potter © Frederick Warne and
Company 1905.

The publishers would also like to
thank the following: David
Austin for cartoons; Ken Pyne
and Catalyst Communications
for Red Star cartoons; Arthur
Sidey and the *Daily Mirror* for
the photograph on p. 139; the
children of Caversham Park
Primary School, Reading, for
their drawings; Jason Harris of St
John's School, Brighton, for his
letter and drawing.

Layout Roger Lightfoot.

Frontispiece: *Les Stocker at his happiest, with two recuperated patients.*

Contents

Acknowledgements

Without the people who bother to pick up sick or injured hedgehogs and bring them to St Tiggywinkles I would not have been able to write this book and many thousands of hedgehogs would have perished.

Throughout my encounters with our prickly friends my wife Sue has helped me through the ups and downs and thrown herself into the orphans' rearing so that at last we can pass on surefire methods of raising baby hedgehogs. Her comments on my writing have made this book even more complete.

Our local veterinary surgeons Richard Hill and Russell Kilshaw, of Tuckett Gray and Partners, have with me pioneered hedgehog treatments and Russell has given up many hours of his valuable free time to work on our patients, take photographs and read my chapters on medical care and drug dosages. A good friend, Norman Glennard MSc, kindly looked at the chapter on garden chemicals; and Kay Lofty and Catherine Cummings can't be thanked enough for the many hours spent typing my manuscript and suffering in silence as I made alterations. Wendy Duggan, Joyce Pope and Les Sharp helped me gather the information I needed for the book, while Mrs J. Stocker in New Zealand, Barbara Head in Alderney and Vivian Naess in Norway informed me about their native hedgehogs. Claudia Perry is doing a great deal to promote hedgehogs in the Southampton area and her collection of 'hedgehogabilia' shows how popular this animal has become. Dr Robert Brockie, Dr Pat Campbell, Chris Dickman, Bob George, John Lamming, Dr Pat Morris, Dr Julian Vincent and Dr D. W. Yalden have all produced papers on hedgehog topics which I have found invaluable not only for this book but during my daily excursions into hedgehog behaviour.

I am grateful to Mr Thomas for allowing me to photograph 'Alice' for this book, and for the help of John Hartley of the Jersey Wildlife Preservation Trust when my great friend Tom Cooper photographed the tenrec. Dr Brian Bartram at London Zoo arranged facilities for me to photograph their desert hedgehogs, an experience which made me fully appreciate the extraordinary patience of Arthur Sidey who has made animal photography such an art.

Ian Mackay's drawings, where no photographs were available, show the scope and character of hedgehog species; and I would like to thank Pam Ayres very much for letting me use her wonderful poem and F. J. M. Chaplin for giving permission to include the 'Hedgehog Hunter'.

The work of St Tiggywinkles goes on with the daily help of young Chris Kirk and Trevor Mayne. Lana Chapman runs our sponsorship scheme for hedgehogs and all our volunteers help to make St Tiggywinkles a success. We could not manage without them or without the support of the British Petroleum Company plc, British Telecom and the Gold Fields Environment Trust. I am particularly grateful, too, to Hedgehog Foods Ltd, producers of a range of organic crisps, who have supported the promotion of this book and the launch of our campaign to Save the Hedgehog.

But, all in all, none of this would have been possible without the strength, fortitude and character of all those hedgehogs.

Foreword

by John Craven

LES STOCKER, his wife Sue and their amazing collection of battered, broken wild creatures first came to my attention through my youngest daughter, Vicky, then aged ten and mad about animals. We live in the Chiltern Hills, not far from the Stockers' wildlife hospital in Aylesbury – a town which, through their efforts, has become what Les calls 'the hedgehog capital of the world'.

Vicky contacted the Stockers to see if she could help in any way and was invited to look round the hospital. Later, I went along too – and found that in the back garden of a modern detached house on an estate there was a whole menagerie of wounded wildlife, being mended with infinite care by Les and Sue. I saw not just hedgehogs but deer, badgers, pigeons, squirrels, mink, rabbits, foxes, a swan, kestrels, owls and lots more, all of them taken or sent to the Wildlife Hospitals Trust after being found injured in many parts of the Kingdom. And the healing was all happening in this extraordinary back garden.

I'm glad to say that the Trust, which also includes the St Tiggywinkles hospital for hedgehogs, will shortly be moving to a purpose-built centre on a new site in Aylesbury, thanks to money raised by generous supporters.

The Craven family readily agreed when Les and Sue asked if some of their hedgehogs – Mrs Tiggy-winkle, no less, with her four babies and two young males – could be released into the wild in our garden. We keep spotting signs of them, and I'm now a devoted hedgehog supporter!

During my television career, I've reported on many threats to wild animals and filmed with giant pandas in China, with tigers in India, and with elephants and rhinos in Africa. But now, literally in my own backyard, there's an unassuming little creature which is also very much in danger.

Something like one hundred thousand hedgehogs are killed on Britain's roads every year, and many more are killed by kindness – by people giving them the wrong kind of food. Now, in this book, Les Stocker tells of his crusade to get the humble hedgehog a better deal. He's a city boy, born in Battersea, and his first-ever sighting of a hedgehog was in Harrods pet shop. He came across his first wild one while pacing the garden of his London home on the night that his son was being born.

Until recent times, he tells us, hedgehogs had a bad public image yet they were innocent of many crimes attributed to them. Under a law of 1566, which was not repealed for three hundred years, a reward of threepence was paid for them, dead or alive. Shakespeare helped to give them a bad name, and they certainly can't climb trees and run off with apples stuck to their spikes, as suggested by the Roman writer Pliny.

What they *can* do with their voracious appetite is get rid of an awful lot of small pests and not so long ago many households kept them as 'below-stairs' servants, to consume cockroaches in the cellars. The British only started to love hedgehogs earlier this century, after Beatrix Potter turned one of them into a washer-woman in *The Tale of Mrs Tiggy-winkle*. Now here is a book that will do as much and more to improve the general image of these strange, spiky creatures and it is a book which is indeed well named. The author presents a mixture of careful scientific and veterinary study, autobiography and fascinating fact, and he's a man who can write of 'Hedgehog Aid' and genuinely mean it. Those injured little patients in St Tiggywinkles hospital owe a great deal to the Stockers.

John Craven 1987

Sue with some of the inmates of St Tiggywinkles (photo Mike Lawn).

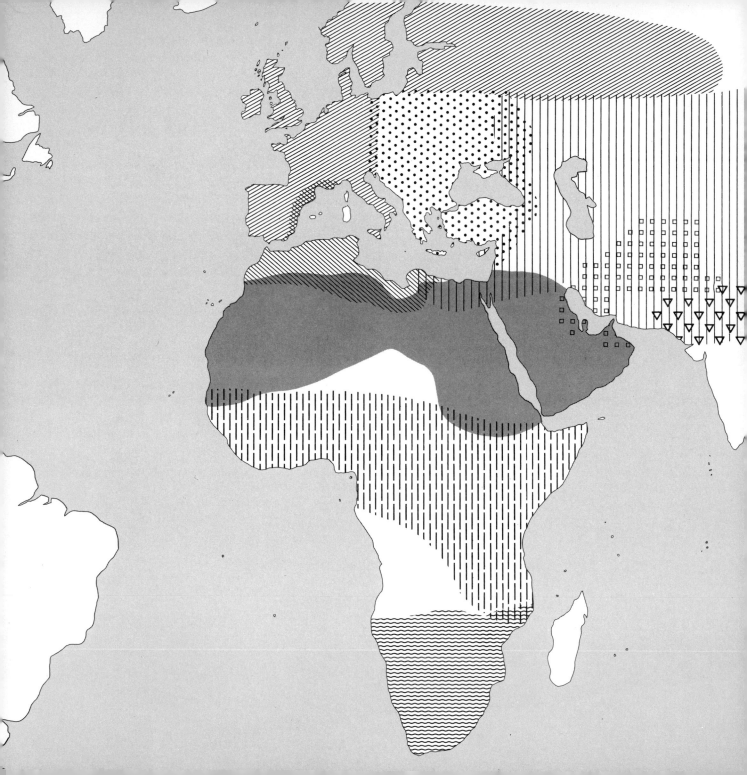

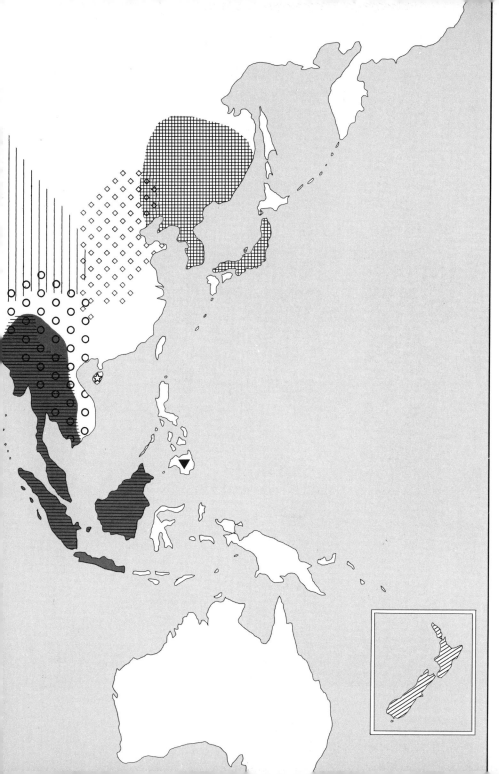

World distribution of hedgehogs

Key

 Hemiechinus dauuricus
DAURIAN HEDGEHOG

 Paraechinus micropus
INDIAN HEDGEHOG

 Paraechinus hypomelas
BRANDT'S HEDGEHOG

 Paraechinus aethiopicus
DESERT HEDGEHOG

 Erinaceus frontalis
CAPE HEDGEHOG

 Erinaceus albiventris
FOUR-TOED HEDGEHOG

 Hemiechinus auritus
LONG-EARED HEDGEHOG

 Erinaceus concolor
EASTERN HEDGEHOG

 Neotetracus sinensis
SHREW HEDGEHOG

 Erinaceus algirus
ALGERIAN HEDGEHOG

 Podogymnura truei
MINDANAO MOON RAT

 Neohylomys hainanensis
HAINAN MOON RAT

 Hylomys suillus
LESSER MOON RAT

Erinaceus amurensis
EASTERN ASIATIC HEDGEHOG

Echinosorex gymnurus
GREATER MOON RAT

Erinaceus europaeus
WESTERN HEDGEHOG

Note: There are no hedgehogs in North and
South America or the arctic regions.

Wincey Willis, Robert Powell and Nick Davis fundraising for St Tiggywinkles (photo Barry Keen, Bucks and Herts Newspapers).

Prologue

THE BARRAGE was ear-shattering as every cameraman, hot for news, captured the moment for his paper. Tape-recorders whirred, television cameras from at least three channels vied for the best vantage points as Susan Hampshire, star of many previous screen classics, cut the silk ribbon. For once the big stars of the animal world, the gorillas, pandas and tigers, were forgotten as at last the hedgehog, so much a part of all our lives, had his day.

It is odd how we take for granted the wild animals which live on our own doorsteps. People put out bread and milk for their visiting hedgehogs yet somehow nobody noticed the animals' plight until, during the drought of 1984, the whole hedgehog population of Britain seemed to be venturing out in the daytime to die right under our noses.

At our wildlife hospital in Aylesbury we had for many years taken in all manner of wildlife casualties but suddenly hedgehogs needed our help. As they were brought to us, sent to us and crawled to us we realised how desperate the situation had become. Yet here we were, a nation of animal lovers – surely Britain could no longer turn its back on hedgehogs?

Of course it couldn't and before long we had every newspaper, radio station and television programme screaming out: 'Look out for your local hedgehog. Does he limp, is he out during the day, does he have enough water to drink?' Within hours our overworked telephone was buzzing.

Then another shock realisation hit home: nobody in the country seemed to know how to treat sick or injured hedgehogs and many veterinarians did not have the time to spend on prickly balls of fleas which would not co-operate as dogs and cats do. We wanted to help but many of the animals were too far away – although some people drove hundreds of miles, through the night, to bring their casualties to us. We asked for British Rail's help and, although red tape threatens the 'Hedgehog Express', many hedgehogs are still being saved by the overnight train journey to Aylesbury station.

At last our prickly friends were no longer being taken for granted, but the deluge of casualties painted an ominous picture for their future. We already had the busiest, yet most confined, of wildlife hospitals but as hedgehog casualties with severe injuries were to be with us for a considerable time we had to make additional arrangements for their housing. As always, fate took a hand. In 1984 a local manufacturer, John Morley of the Gatemakers, stepped forward with the offer of a smart timber structure to serve as a ward for hedgehog patients.

Susan Hampshire officially opens St Tiggywinkles – the world's first hedgehog hospital unit.

This was to be more than just a ward; it was to be the only centre in the world catering exclusively for sick or injured hedgehogs, a genuine hedgehog hospital. Many human hospital counterparts donated surplus medical equipment; the British Petroleum Company provided our first incubator; the specially designed cages were ready for occupation.

Our hedgehog hospital was to be as important to the animal world as St Bartholomew's Hospital in London is to humans. We christened it St Tiggywinkles in honour of Beatrix Potter's famous washer-woman hedgehog, Mrs Tiggy-winkle, who has done so much to endear hedgehogs to the children of the world.

Just then, as if to endorse all our efforts, we heard that our campaign to save hedgehogs had won a Conservation Foundation Award. We were to be presented with the award by Miss Susan Hampshire and Mr Paddy Mitchell of Trust House Forte, the sponsors of the award. We asked if Miss Hampshire would also do us the honour of officially opening St Tiggywinkles.

Susan did more than that. She and two other famous actors, Colin Baker and Bill Oddie, spent a great day, 9th August 1985, sharing the limelight with the hedgehogs, and exchanging hedgehog reminiscences. This was the hedgehog's day: no longer would it have to cry out unheard.

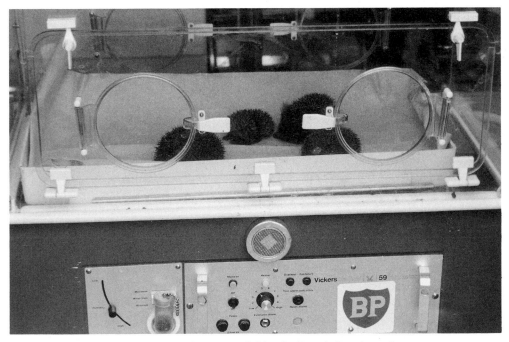

Our first hedgehog incubator provided by the British Petroleum Company.

Close Encounters

GROPING THROUGH the yellow silent smog of a London street, on a typical autumn evening in the 1950s, I found it hard to imagine that there were such things as hedgehogs. Certainly I had never seen a wild one although there were always plenty of those giant yellow slugs about, which they were supposed to relish. The salt pot was the predator the slugs feared, with grubby sparrows and pigeons the only wildlife to witness their passing. These town birds had evolved an existence relying on man's scraps and not on the supply of insects which is the mainstay of most bird-breeding populations. The only trees, the long-suffering planes, regularly had to cast their bark to rid themselves of the soot and grime.

But why on earth was I interested? Here was I, a town boy from the depths of dark-grey Battersea, streetwise to the concrete jungle but never having been into a truly wild wood or had any contact with the birds and animals which, my books told me, lived there. Yet, somehow, by my last years at primary school I knew all about these – their names, habits, description – and I was confident that I would recognise them instantly, if ever I were to see any of them.

I seemed to soak up any information on the subject. Even the few books which I had were chosen because they dealt with the animals and birds of the countryside.

By the time I was ten years old I could identify and talk about any animal picture I saw. When my form mistress started a series of natural history lessons, I was in my element. I seemed to know all the answers but when the practical lessons started, my euphoria was dampened. One particular weekend project, I remember vividly, required us to go out and collect as many 'fruits of the field' as we could. Combing every inch of Clapham Common I managed to amass some plane 'bobs' and a few sycamore 'helicopters'. There wasn't anything else. Yet when we went back to class on Monday, those boys and girls whose parents owned cars had been out to the countryside and had collections of every shape, colour and size: acorns, ash keys, medlars, beech mast, hazel nuts and berries, some of which I had never seen before. To me that countryside seemed to be a world away but at least I had the consolation that my plane 'bobs' made superb itching powder.

Undaunted, the sleeping giant of my wildlife interest continued to flourish. I found my own countryside on Wimbledon Common and every Saturday morning my sixpence pocket money allowed me to catch the 168 bus to that magic place. Hour after hour I would trek across the heaths, woods and rides of my wilderness. The tower blocks that now scar the Wimbledon skyline were still just an architect's pipe-dream. There was nobody there; the birds and animals had it to themselves. My *Observer's Book of Wild Animals* and my *Observer's Book of British Birds* had never been so well thumbed but, although I spotted many of the birds, the only wild animals I saw were squirrels and an occasional deer – except one day when I investigated a rustle in a tuft of grass and discovered my first lizard.

At home I had taken over the disused chicken runs at the bottom of the backyard. Tidied up, and with the door rehung, my den was soon full of treasures found on my excursions. There was an odd collection of containers stacked neatly against the back wall: cigar boxes full of old birds' nests, and date boxes holding one or two sparrow's eggs found scattered on the roof of the school. Matchboxes held bugs and those old biscuit tins with hinged glass lids made an excellent home for several types of caterpillar whose frass gave the den its typical insect aroma. My pride and joy was a menacing but dead stag beetle I had found on the Common. I never did find a live one but even a dead one proved very effective for terrorising two younger sisters. My most dastardly deed, however, was to save up my pocket money and splash out on a grass snake, which cost me four shillings at a local pet shop. Nobody around had ever seen a real, live British snake so he became the centre of interest at those natural history lessons. Looking back, I now see how unfair it was to keep a wild animal in captivity, although I eventually tried to redeem myself by releasing it on a large, grassy bomb site.

I had so much freedom during those primary school days and when the other pupils elected me

as Head Boy I had the licence to make regular visits to the pigeons' and sparrows' nests on the school roof behind the art room. I even found injured pigeons but they never survived. As there were not many cars in London, I met few road casualties on my way home from school. I picked one up, however, and took it cushioned under my jumper on the bus to the People's Dispensary for Sick Animals in Wandsworth, only to be told that I had been nursing a dead pigeon. Thankfully my techniques have improved since then.

Those halcyon days at primary school came to an end when I passed the eleven plus and won a scholarship to a local public school. The more intensive teaching at Emanuel School in Wandsworth meant that I would have plenty of 'prep' to do after school. Everything there was different: 'prep' meant homework; you needed an 'aegrotat' to be ill and an 'exeat' to leave school during the day. The playground was the 'quad', but the 'field' was a playing field surrounded by grass and trees which allowed me some contact with wild birds. Once a year I found myself, even then, doing a bit of wildlife rescue. Deep in the grounds was the rowing tank where we practised when we could not go on the Thames at Putney. One particular female mallard always built her nest in its depths and then found that she could not get her brood up onto dry land. In the past, no doubt they had drowned, but now help was at hand.

Marooned as it was between two sets of main railway lines into Clapham Junction, Emanuel was a train-spotters' paradise, with most of the younger

Feeding a hedgehog.

pupils spending every spare minute recording the complicated sets of numbers on the great steam locomotives. I never got that bug but preferred meandering through the trees watching the comings and goings of real creepy crawlies.

I suppose it was the fact of getting a place at this school which was indirectly responsible for my obsession with the enigma of the hedgehog. Emanuel School insisted on every boy wearing a school uniform that could only be bought at Harrods. Looking back I realise that my parents must have made sacrifices in order to send me to Emanuel, but I was too excited to appreciate this when we made the journey to Harrods to order my dark grey, short-trousered, first-year uniform. As Mother paid the bill, I took the opportunity to investigate the irresistible departmental sign which said 'Zoo'. After an interminable trek through the great store I eventually found the animals' section and there, for sale, saw my first live hedgehogs. I resisted the temptation to buy one – I could never have afforded the asking price in any case.

I did fairly well at school but, not surprisingly, shone at biology. I managed to master most of the intricacies of school life but am still baffled as to how, when my biology marks averaged 96 per cent, I was put into the classics and economics stream where I was forced to say goodbye to all the sciences. As an adolescent in those days, you did as you were told, so after passing my O-levels, without even sitting the biology exam, I was pigeon-holed by the Careers Master for a career in accountancy.

Signed up under Articles for five years, I had to attend college in the City on three nights a week and had scarcely any spare time. When eventually I managed to pass the accountancy exams, I had some money in my pocket at last. Not a lot, but

in hand-made 'winklepickers' and fashionable suits with all the latest accoutrements, every Saturday night was party night.

My wildlife enthusiasm dimmed for a time except when occasionally I ventured to the coast and it was immediately revived. Mind you, even during those days at the seaside I never saw a hedgehog. Probably my approaching heavy townie footsteps sent them all scurrying for cover. In fact, I still saw none of the animals described in my *Observer's Book* but the variety of birds and butterflies made up for this. Nonetheless, these 'away-days' were the highlights of my year. I never got over the gleaming iridescence of starlings, which were never seen in London then – they had me imagining 'bee eater' and 'humming bird' – and once, on a trip to Clacton, I even heard a corncrake. Not that I could see one, but at least I knew it was there.

How different it is now: the clean, green glory that was our countryside has lost its wildlife to the insidious pesticides that have cut the foodchain at its source. The new soot-free cities are fast becoming the only haven for wild animals and birds.

Fate has a way of leading the way when it comes to looking after animals. One Saturday night at a party a young lady needed a 'knight in shining armour'. I tried to fit the bill as best I could and was rewarded by being allowed to escort her home to Chelsea. To Sue I was a fashionably dressed but gentlemanly party-goer; little did she realise that under that exterior was an eccentric driving force.

She may have had an inkling, as our romance blossomed, when she heard that one night after leaving her and cycling home along the Chelsea Embankment I came across six abandoned kittens. Stuffing them down my sweater I took them home with me. In the morning my mother came into my room and must have despaired to see that the obsession which had been part of my childhood was still simmering under the surface. She may even have warned Sue whom by now I was dragging across Richmond Park and Box Hill, bombarding her with information about every bird or plant we saw. At my parents' home I had discovered the intricacies of propagating exotic cacti and garden plants. My aquariums of tropical fish became a focal point. Now I seemed to have even less time to take Sue dancing. But she persevered and four years later at the splendid church in Redcliffe Gardens, Kensington, we were married.

Our first married home was a two-roomed flat in Raynes Park. We did not have easy access to a garden and when I blew out all the windows trying to light the antique bath heater we had to find somewhere else to live. We were lucky. We managed to take on the tenancy of a maisonette just up the road, across the Kingston by-pass, backing on to Malden Golf Course. Of course this rekindled all my wild memories, and I am not sure that Sue knew what had hit her.

I spent every waking moment in the garden, transforming it from a mud pile to a picture-book landscape. In the pond I had fish, frogs and newts, and the bird table was always alive with blue tits, woodpeckers, nuthatches and jays. When we had an idyllic Devon holiday one summer amongst the teeming gull colony, the chicks succeeded in winning Sue over. After that she too started to spend hours in the garden and wandering the golf course. There I found all the animals I had never seen – squirrels, rabbits, foxes and Sue's favourites, a family of wood mice living under our strawberry patch.

We had just joined the affluent few who owned a car. We made regular trips into the countryside to see more wildlife, but there wasn't any there. Not only did we not see any animals but the birds and butterflies were hard to find: the poisons had taken their toll. To discover a bird's nest was a major achievement; there was only field after field of boring cereals and definitely *no hedgehogs*.

Thank goodness, we felt, that the new roads could rush us back to London. Probably the wild animals used the same routes to the metropolis but, keeping to the safe corridors of the grass verges, found a traffic-free pathway to new sources of untainted food. We hurried straight out on to the golf course at the bottom of the garden, with its resident kestrel patrolling the rough, rabbits gambolling in the woodland edge; there were birds' nests in every bush, there was ivy, bramble and traveller's joy hiding the lost golf balls, and every evening there was the long eerie serenade of the invisible tawny owls. Mind you, London's pollution still persisted in the brook that ran through the green: almost nothing grew or swam or wriggled in those deceptively clear poisoned waters, where only the brown rats managed to survive.

Yet it was nearby, in our garden, that at last I met my first hedgehogs. I will never forget the date, 8th July 1968, because it was the night before our son Colin was born. Getting in the way of the doctor and the midwives and having boiled every kettle within reach, I was exiled to the balcony to share the night with the tawnies around the ninth green. Nobody else was around as I listened to the rustle of a mouse and her family under the strawberries; the last train to Clapham Junction rattled in the distance. Suddenly a tremendous snorting exploded by the back gate. Hardly daring to investigate I crept towards the swaying, snorting bean patch. Switching on my torch, then banging it to make it work, I was just in time to see two hedgehogs leap apart and scuttle into the flower borders. I had always thought that hedgehogs were slow ambling creatures but these two were gone in an instant. Quickly I followed their direction towards the golf course but they had become just a fast disappearing rustle under the thicket of bramble and forsythia at the bottom of the garden.

Hurrying back inside I wanted to tell Sue of my close encounter but at that moment she was not interested. A few hours later I heard, coming from the nursery, another new sound which thrilled me even more: the sound of a newborn baby's first cries. What a night!

Over the next few weeks I had to leave my hedgehog quest and found time only to put out nightly bowls of bread and milk. Each morning the bowl was licked clean and invariably turned upside down. It must have been done by hedgehogs but little did I know then that the pasteurised milk was doing them no good at all. Only when the household had settled back to normal could I resume my nightly searches for the evasive hedgehogs. During the day I quartered every inch of the garden (and it seemed the golf course) for signs of hedgehog activity.

I had read that both male and female hedgehogs would build themselves nests approximately the size of footballs and that pregnant females would

A hedgehog will collect nest material in its mouth and will even pluck grass to make its own hay.

construct nurseries which were even larger. With simple ingenuity the hedgehog collects, in its mouth, clumps of grass, fallen leaves or even the old newspapers. It gathers its gleanings into a heap under a dense hedge, bramble thicket or intended bonfire. Then it merely dives into the centre of the heap and turns round and round, literally using its spines to comb the nest lining into position. Easily made, these summer nests are only used for a few days until the hedgehog decides to move out, when it quickly builds another home elsewhere. If they find a nest vacated by another hedgehog, they will not hesitate to move in, sometimes even returning to their own previously discarded nests.

Nursery nests, in use from May each year, are similar though a little more diligently constructed and often larger (up to 50 centimetres in diameter) in order to accommodate six or seven youngsters. They are frequently built into compost or manure heaps where the natural warmth of the decomposing vegetable matter no doubt helps keep the young 'piglets' warm when their mother is out foraging on chilly nights and where the teeming invertebrate life makes easy pickings for a busy hedgehog.

Assuming that both these types of nest would be easy to find under brambles or other bushes I took out a small bag of flour that I could sprinkle around to register any hedgehog comings and goings. I had

A nest of pin-cushions.

23

no intention of searching inside the nests in case I were to disturb a nursing mother. Female hedgehogs are notorious for destroying their offspring if they are disturbed.

I had seen two hedgehogs on that first night and, knowing from my reading about their solitary nesting behaviour, I could assume that there would be at least two nests somewhere on the golf course. All I found, well hidden under an old domestic oil tank buried in the undergrowth, was the remains of an old winter nest. Hedgehogs construct these hibernacula under sheds or beneath the cavernous root systems of old trees. Rabbit burrows or log piles also give some protection from the weather to hibernating hedgehogs and, although the nest is made in a similar way to the summer nests, the leaf lining is combed and recombed until the leaves overlap and form a waterproof chamber perfectly fitting the dimensions of the hedgehog and giving good insulation against the severest cold. Hedgehogs always build new winter nests, never relying on the efficiency of an old nest even though they may change their situation once or twice during a cold winter.

They always pick a sound weatherproof situation for the winter nests, although the hedgehog I found, many years later, hibernating in a black plastic sack was taking a chance on being carted off to the rubbish dump. It's always worth checking open plastic sacks of garden rubbish for hedgehog intruders. Usually, however, the winter nest is built in a more secure position and as a credit to their construction many last for months after the dormant has left. Looking at the old nest, I could see from its decayed state that the tenant had left months before; it was not worth even scattering a light dusting of flour to register the footprints of any visitor.

I never found a 'live' nest either on the golf course or in the garden, which made me wonder how the dubious gypsy hedgehog hunter of old ever made a living. John Chaplin wrote of his prowess for the Gypsy Lore Society:

He would be seen, jumping up and down, trampling the brambles in the roadside ditch with his heavy nailed boots. Somehow apart from ordinary men, he seemed to belong to wildlife with some sixth sense guiding him to the nest of the 'hotchi-pig' under the bush.

The hedgehog hunter (by John Chaplin, from an original drawing).

I am relieved his heinous profession has become extinct while there are still some hedgehogs left. Every other world species which has become extinct in the last thousand years has done so at the hands of hunters. Yet no doubt his fieldcraft would have helped me to find hedgehogs; he could probably have made sense of the little heaps of mammal droppings which must have offered so many clues to anyone who could interpret them. Still, the quantity and variety of types did confirm that our golf course had become one of the richest wildlife habitats in that part of London.

An animal's droppings can be a great help in establishing the presence of a species. Take the otter's, for instance: people rarely see otters but their 'spraints', left on prominent rocky positions, give researchers the only information as to their numbers or well-being on any particular water system. Droppings contain not only mucus, dead cells from the alimentary canal and bacteria but also the remains of indigestible food that would, I hoped, tell me what and where my quarry had been eating.

Hedgehog faeces are deposited at random not in one place like the thin typically carnivore droppings of the stoat or weasel. Foxes mark on a raised hummock or rock while badgers always use the same latrine hole in the ground. Since rabbits and deer

Hedgehog dropping (actual size).

leave little pellets I had only to differentiate between hedgehogs and carnivores. Hedgehogs' faeces are usually 3 to 4 centimetres long and about 1 centimetre thick. They are sometimes pointed at one end but not with the exaggerated taper of the carnivores. Literally reflecting a preferred diet of beetles, earwigs and other insects a hedgehog's dropping is usually black, speckled with the glistening chitinous remains of wing cases and the elytra of beetles. Just to confuse matters they occasionally munch their way through a dead mouse or bird, leaving their droppings full of hair, feather and bone with no shiny bits; just a grey, dull, drawn-out pellet rather like the weasel's. As they were typically deposited singly and at random, I decided the samples I had found were definitely hedgehog's.

Even I could tell that hedgehogs had been foraging in my strawberry patch. Knowing that they will occasionally eat fruit I was prepared to find some undigested particles in the faeces but no, my hedgehogs seemed to be thriving on the mass of 'creepy crawlies' which were really guilty of eating the strawberries.

I was quite pleased with my detective work so far but my next find, although definitely proving the presence of hedgehogs, undermined my excitement: trapped in the bottom of a chain-link fence on the railway embankment were the small skull and various pieces of bone of what must have been a hedgehog but not, I hoped, one of the two I had seen. I knew not to touch dead animal matter for fear of any lingering bacteria so I went back to fetch a pair of rubber gloves in order to collect all I could. It was hard to tell if the skeleton was complete so I also gathered some of the soil from beneath it. Taking all this back home I gently washed it under a running tap to remove any soil particles and to extract from the soil any small bones or teeth. I still dared not handle the pieces so I soaked them for a few hours in a strong solution of household bleach to kill any remaining germs. When I had rinsed them again and dried them I was able to set about definitely identifying the skeleton.

The length of the skull, which measured 58 millimetres, put it well within the accepted hedgehog range of 54 to 64 millimetres. Its width of 35 millimetres was once again within the guidelines of 32 to 39 millimetres. As with all British wild mammal skulls, except the powerfully-jawed badger, the lower jaw bones had fallen away from the top jaw, and many of the teeth were now scattered at the bottom of my cleaning dish. Each tooth fitted exactly into its own socket and with a dab of glue on each there was no fear of them falling out again. All 36 teeth were there, so by a process of elimination I could confirm my identification. There were none of the scissor-like shearing teeth of the carnivore; instead the teeth were small like an insectivore's but without the sharper points of the mole's teeth. The mole has large canine teeth whereas the hedgehog's are hardly noticeable; the mole uses its canines to impale its prey, while the hedgehog relies on its first incisors to scoop up beetles, caterpillars and other invertebrates. This skull had very prominent first incisors which could have easily been mistaken for canine teeth.

All the teeth together showed the typical hedgehog dental formula of six incisors, two canines, six pre-molars and six molars in the top jaw, and four incisors, two canines, four pre-molars and six molars in the bottom jaw, just as they were shown in school scientific textbooks. Although pointed, the skull was somewhat shorter than that of other insectivores and had wider strong cheekbones. Definitely a hedgehog,

I decided, but one which like so many had perished hopelessly entangled in mesh.

I had already established that, in spite of the casualty, there was a healthy hedgehog population on the golf course but I still couldn't be sure of seeing them when they were out and about on their nightly forays. If like other mammals they used good regular trackways which I could identify, I would be able to watch them under a red light which would be invisible to the colour-blind hedgehogs. I might even be able to establish just how many there were in our area. So far I had not found any hedgehog footprints, not even in the soft mud created by the golfers on their way up to the footbridge over the brook. However, there were numerous little worn animal paths through the long green edges leading to gaps under fences and hedges. A layer of fine damp soil laid on these pathways would show me which were in use and which were not.

Hedgehogs have flat feet or, to put it more scientifically, are plantigrade, that is they put the whole of their foot to the ground. This betrays their ancestry which goes back to days long before such modifications as cloven hooves and paws had evolved. They, like all the primitive insectivores, have five toes on

Right Fore Leg

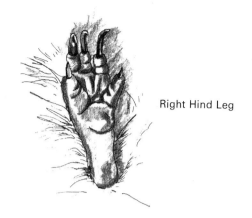

Right Hind Leg

fast will put his back feet completely over or even in front of the fore feet impressions so that the crucial fifth toe will not leave any mark whatsoever. But close inspection of its wavy trail, with footprints 6 centimetres apart, will show that a hedgehog's front feet turn slightly inward while its back feet turn outwards – showing the toes and claws on each foot to good effect. Sprinkling some fine damp soil on the tracks I got some good sets of hedgehog prints, together with those of wood mice, a weasel and a small bird's, probably the ground-loving blackbird.

All set up with a red light on miles of extension cables I maintained nightly vigils over my chosen trackway. Hedgehogs came and went, some large, some small, some hurrying, some ambling along snuffling every blade of grass. But was it just one or two hedgehogs leading me a merry dance or was it five or six or even more? I didn't want to mark them in any way so my plan to do a local census of hedgehogs had to be scrapped; but it seemed reasonable to assume that our urban neighbourhood of gardens, parks, embankments, cemeteries and roadside verges supported a healthy population of hedgehogs large and small.

each foot (although there is one hedgehog species *Erinaceus albiventris* from Africa which has only four toes on its hind feet).

The impressions of an adult hedgehog's feet are approximately 2.5 centimetres long by about 2.8 centimetres broad compared with the hind feet which are 3 centimetres long by only 2 centimetres broad. Their length of stride is between 10 and 15 centimetres and the track can be between 3 and 6 centimetres wide, again depending on the age and size of the animal. They have very prominent pads on their feet which can give a good impression if the conditions are right.

All this sounds very helpful until you put on your Indian scout hat and go out to find a trail. Firstly, hedgehogs tend to avoid wet or muddy places where open sections could give a good record of passing animal traffic. Don't worry, they will leave their marks on the edge of muddy puddles or in damp woodland edges, but to confuse you, the impressions of their back feet encroach onto the front feet impressions so that the prints of their long back claws reach the prints of the front pads. To add to the confusion you may find that a hedgehog walking

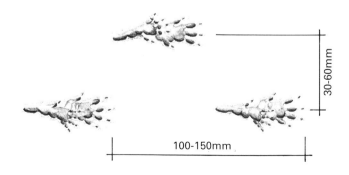

30-60mm

100-150mm

Typical hedgehog tracks (to scale).

Although I used the word healthy, it was at this period that I met my first live hedgehog casualty and soon realised that nothing at all had been done to cater for the needs of wild animals in trouble.

I am sure that my neighbours had me marked down as some sort of nut, sitting on the golf course night after night, watching hedgehogs, but when one was found stranded during the day, they knew where to come. There, curled up in the middle of an immaculate lawn, was a fairly large hedgehog. Gingerly I sidled up to it but it made no attempt to get away. I bent down to touch it; still no movement, though it was breathing. I had never picked up a hedgehog before but its spines were not as painful as I had imagined. Carrying it home I could see that it was obviously very seriously injured and to my horror I found that its underside was a seething mass of maggots. Somehow I managed not to drop it but got it into the garage to see if there was anything I could do. I couldn't kill it but I had to do something to stop its torture. A dish of Dettol and a pair of tweezers seemed a good idea but as I picked out one maggot, another two reared their ugly heads. A bath of Dettol? No good, the maggots seemed to have passed right through its body. A quick reference to my meagre library of animal case books suggested giving it glucose to drink. What good would that do? I felt helpless. Thankfully, the hedgehog died shortly afterwards and I made sure that every last maggot suffered a similar fate.

I hadn't been able to save the animal, but could anybody have done more, I wondered. That afternoon made me realise that hedgehogs are not just bundles of spikes and fleas which eat slugs, but that they suffer pain just as we do, and the experience made me determined that next time I found an injured animal I should know what to do. From that moment my collection of animal case books steadily increased. I spent hours in libraries and bookshops searching for the smattering of information which was available. If there was to be a next time, I wanted to be prepared.

Lindsey Durrant

The Hedgehog Comes of Age

I HAD to learn more about hedgehogs. This was the only wild animal that would come unafraid into my garden, as he has gone into thousands of gardens, but nobody seemed to know anything about his needs or even his likes or dislikes. There must be books, I thought, on our most familiar animal. After all, everybody knows what a hedgehog looks like, even if they have never heard of a fat-tailed dormouse or a Reeves muntjac.

Yes, there were a few books – such as *Animals as Friends* and *With Nature and a Camera* – but as I read deeper and deeper the horror of our mistreatment of hedgehogs began to sink in. There were so many fallacies about their lifestyle, it seemed a miracle that they had survived man's persecution over the centuries.

You could understand the early British hunter-gatherers of the Mesolithic period, ten thousand years ago, relying on the ambling hedgehog as food which was easily caught, but when you read that among the hedgehog bones found as table scraps there were bones of the elk, aurochs, wild boar, beaver and wolf, all now extinct in Britain, you begin to realise that hedgehogs have done well to survive this far. Of the Mesolithic *table d'hôte* remains in Star Carr in Yorkshire the pine marten is just hanging onto existence in this country with only the

fox, by his dexterity, and the badger, by his secrecy, having fought successfully shoulder to shoulder with the hedgehog into the twentieth century.

How the hedgehog, or urchone, as he was then known, managed to prosper is amazing. No doubt many were eaten by the ancient Britons but when you discover that hedgehog was still appearing on the menu at feasts in the fifteenth century you begin to marvel at its resilience, particularly since the hedgehog was also at risk from the medical men who regarded certain parts of the animal as a cure for various maladies which affected man. As long ago as 1350 Konrad of Megenberg told how the flesh of the hedgehog was good for the stomach. Three hundred years later Edward Topsell's seventeenth-century manuscript, *Historie of Four-footed*

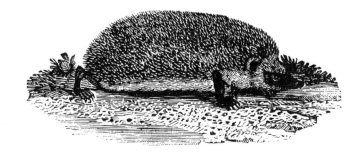

Eighteenth-century wood engraving by Thomas Bewick.

29

Beasts, extolled a hedgehog's virtues against colic as well as baldness, boils, stones; this list is endless but hardly pertinent to our interest in hedgehogs except for one other cure that was as horrific as it was gruesome: eating the fried right eye of a hedgehog was supposed to help one see in the dark.

The Romans used dried hedgehog skins to card out wool but those were more barbaric times; there is no excuse for the more recent practice of horsemen who used skins to prod their mounts over show-jumps or to keep carriage horses on a straight course.

Fortunately, however, there have always been a few observers interested in the hedgehog simply as a wild animal whose habits were worth studying. As early as the fourth century BC, Aristotle was writing in Greece of the 'echinus' that 'moved from one wall to another according to the direction of the wind'. Whether his observations had any basis in fact did not seem to matter, and, as with so many hedgehog 'antiquities', the story has been updated on more than one occasion.

Albert the Great, the Dominican scholar of the thirteenth century, expanded the theory by telling how 'the hedgehog makes three or four exits to its lair or dwelling and when it senses that the wind is going to blow from a certain direction, it closes the corresponding hole'. He goes on to explain how hedgehogs have two anal holes – quite unlike other animals and, of course, totally incorrect. The British later elaborated the legend in an old farming manual but, as with all handed-down stories, Albert's four exits and two anal holes seem to have been confused: 'The hedgehog commonly hath two holes or vents in his den or cave, the one towards the south and the other towards the north; and look which of them he stops thence will great storms and winds follow.'

The Romans had had their own form of hedgehog weather forecast; noticing that hedgehogs hibernated, they formulated the fallacy that is still celebrated in many parts of the world:

> If during hibernation, he [the hedgehog] looks out of his den on 2nd February and sees his shadow it means there is a clear moon and six more weeks of winter so he returns to his burrow.

It may be confusing that 2nd February turns out to be the strictly Christian festival of Candlemas, which, in the fifth century replaced the original Roman Festival of Februa. The Christians kept their own version of the weather prediction, dispensing with the hedgehog:

> If Candlemas be fair,
> There be two winters in the year.

But St Dubricius the fifth-century saint is shown, on a stained-glass window in Hentland Church, in Gloucestershire, with a hedgehog at his feet. Did later Christians, I wonder, retain some part of the old legend?

Although the superstition barely survives in Britain, the people of Wiarton in Canada have taken the hedgehog barometer to their hearts. As they have no hedgehogs in North America the indigenous ground hog, a furry rodent, has been substituted and every Candlemas weekend 'Wiarton Willie' ventures forth with his weather prediction for the town Mayor. The Americans in Pennsylvania, just across the border from Ontario, in fact lay claim to the idea of substituting a ground hog for a hedgehog and 'Punxsutawney Phil' still comes out on 2nd February.

This friendly rivalry does no harm to the hedgehog or the ground hog and so far none of these fallacies have caused the hedgehog any problems. What is surprising is that such myths still persist, even though it is obvious that they have no basis in fact. A well known story by Pliny the Elder, in his *Historia Naturalis*, told how hedgehogs climbed trees in order to knock off the apples and pears. The hedgehog would, he wrote,

> Then throw itself down upon them so that the fruit may stick to his spines and gaily trots off with its prize.

Although an accomplished observer, I think that Pliny himself must take the prize for imagination and for starting one of the lengthiest time-wasters ever. His assertions of hedgehog 'scrumping' prowess have outlasted much of the rest of his writings, and his revelations about the tree-climbing hedgehogs were even confirmed by the English clergyman and writer, Edward Topsell, in the seventeenth century.

Amazingly, every hedgehog book since (including this one) has carried the story. What is more worrying is that many scientists have gone to great lengths to prove Pliny right but, of course, nobody has ever witnessed the great hedgehog act. They have shown that an apple stuck on a spine by force will stay there and that hedgehogs might accidentally pick one up, but the exercise is pointless: hedgehogs do not eat much fruit and certainly would not go out of their way to carry any off. By studying live hedgehogs one can see that when they are foraging their spines lie flat and relaxed. Only when they are alarmed do they flex their armour, which they can only do by curling their heads under and then rolling up – in no position to see or scent where the nearest apple or pear would be. Pliny was nearer reality than any modern theories, in that if a hedgehog were to drop, either accidentally or intentionally,

Hedgehog with its spines laid flat.

from a height, it would curl up into a spine-flexed ball in order to absorb the impact. But, on the other hand, hedgehogs cannot climb trees.

In medieval Britain, people believed that hedgehogs could suckle milk from cows' udders, and great faith was put in Old Nancy, a fairy who 'for a piece of cake and a bottle of home-brewed ale, would find lost iron plough-pins and prevent hedgehogs from sucking the cows at night-time'. If Old Nancy did not succeed, it seems that hedgehogs were slaughtered anyway, by the thousand. It was even worse in Ireland, where hedgehogs were supposedly witches in animal form, 'graineeogs' or ugly ones that not only suckled the milk from cows but also bewitched them and made their milk dry up.

Farmers did not hesitate to persecute the 'prickly back otchuns' which they believed milked their cows, and the Elizabethan parliament of 1566 even passed laws putting a dead or alive reward of threepence on the head of any hedgehog unlucky enough to be caught.

With so many fallacies stacked up against them the future looked grim for hedgehogs, and when William Shakespeare jumped on the 'hedgehogs are vermin' bandwagon, the whole world came to despise them. Shakespeare described Richard III as a 'hedgehog', obviously meaning something verminous:

> Dost thou grant me hedgehog? Then God grant
> me too
> Thou mayst be damnèd for the wicked deed!

Then later in *A Midsummer Night's Dream* he slandered not only hedgehogs but other animals of the countryside:

> You spotted snakes with double tongue,
> Thorny hedgehogs, be not seen;
> Newts and blindworms, do no wrong;
> Come not near our Fairy Queen.

Nothing was going right for the hedgehog; even his old English name, of urchone or urchin, meant a kind of elf or troublesome sprite. At least Shakespeare, by popularising the word 'hedgehog', helped in a small way to alleviate that slight on the animal's character.

The sixteenth-century bounty hunters would have been paid with silver coins as there was no copper or bronze coin of the realm. Even though it was illegal, many trading companies over the next hundred years started to mint their own copper trade tokens to serve as small change. Thomas Martin

Seventeenth- and eighteenth-century tokens showing heraldic hedgehogs.

of Southwark had a hedgehog emblazoned on the reverse of his coins; and later, at the end of the eighteenth century, a token halfpenny issued at Birmingham in 1793 shows a splendid heraldic shield festooned with five 'hedgehogs guardant passant'.

Even the church joined in the hue and cry, offering its own rewards for hedgehogs killed in churchyards and pinning grisly corpses to the church doors. One parish alone recorded paying out for a thousand corpses in five years and all over the country hedgehog hunting was good business. In seventeenth-century Cheshire a penny per corpse was the bounty, while further north in Westmorland twopence could be earned for every success. Even in the last century, Bedfordshire and Oxford were still paying out their fourpences. It took another Act of Parliament, in 1863, to repeal the law passed three hundred years before. I wonder how many 'prickly back otchuns' perished in all those years. I like to think that the Act was repealed because the case against the hedgehog was proved unfounded, but it was probably because the bounties were costing the government too much.

The myth still persists, if not with the same devastating consequences. I have read of experiments to see if a hedgehog, stretching on its hind legs like a circus elephant, could reach the teats of a standing cow, or if he would willingly take milk from an artificial teat. We all know that hedgehogs will willingly lap up cow's milk, despite the fact that it disagrees with them, and no doubt relish any which is spilled from the overfilled udder of a recumbent cow or offered in any form of man-made receptacle. However, I am not persuaded that the report in the *Veterinary Journal* of May and June 1967, recording hedgehog-like teeth marks on cows' teats, confirms that the animals are milk stealers. Rather, I believe that the hedgehog involved was perpetrating a far more difficult manoeuvre — that of actually trying to eat part of the cow. I know it may sound ludicrous, but hedgehogs have a single-minded determination when it comes to food. I have seen hedgehogs eating a full-grown pigeon, attacking ducks and on one memorable occasion have had to rescue a Canada goose which had a hedgehog firmly gripping its undercarriage. It took some effort to dislodge that hedgehog, so I would not be surprised if the cow under attack had difficulty shaking off its attacker — causing the lacerations reported in the *Veterinary Journal*. Luckily, our forefathers seemed unaware of the hedgehog's meat-eating propensities, but I wonder if their additional reputation of having a venomous bite could be the result of hedgehog bite wounds becoming infected.

Quick to seize the opportunity to clear even more indigenous wild animals from their estates, the gamekeepers took advantage of the bounty schemes and laid another charge against the hedgehog – that

of egg-stealing. Their expertise at trapping, killing and gibbeting hedgehogs earned many of them extra pocket money. In one particular parish in Norfolk, gamekeepers were paid 5s 6d a year to kill any hedgehogs that ventured into Foulsham Churchyard.

True, hedgehogs do break into the occasional pheasant's egg, but generally one that is already cracked, and surveys have shown that their minor depredations represent only a fraction of the losses caused by careless farm workers – and I hope that none of the latter were gibbeted for their actions. Even today, gamekeepers manage to get away with slaughtering hedgehogs. In the privacy of their estates nobody sees what is going on and in Britain there is no law to prevent this slaughter. As recently as 1976 a scientific research programme was carried out on over 100 hedgehogs killed on one estate in East Anglia. No wonder the locality was kept a closely guarded secret. Their estate managed to slaughter about 260 hedgehogs each year until 1969. The only figures available after that date are those already quoted for the 1976 massacre.

When the hedgehog is accused of raiding chicken houses, the rumours have plainly grown out of hand. It is a physical impossibility for a hedgehog to crack a chicken's egg: one researcher even left a hedgehog for a week with no other food available than an egg, which it still did not manage to break. In fact it showed no interest whatsoever in the feast under its nose. Traps and snares continued to be put down. I have even read one report of how a writer heard a hedgehog screaming, caught by one leg in a tortuous, and thankfully now illegal, gin trap. As the trap was in a chicken enclosure he made no attempt to rescue the animal and walked away with the hedgehog's pitiful screaming still ringing in his ears.

33

In the past, there seemed to be only one reason for keeping hedgehogs alive and that was to incarcerate them 'below stairs' where they could earn their keep by killing cockroaches which infested many of the older houses. Only one hundred years ago hedgehogs could be bought quite easily in Leadenhall Market in London. The cellar hedgehog may have had a fairly comfortable if confined life, living for many years and apparently growing fat on a diet of kitchen scraps and, presumably, the occasional cockroach.

The hedgehog has not always been persecuted, however: perhaps the ancient Chinese civilisation was showing us the way when the people of the He Bei Province regarded their resident hedgehogs as sacred. It was not until 1833 that a European spoke up for hedgehogs, when Professor Lorenz Oken suggested in his *General Natural History* that 'they should be protected as useful animals because they devour a lot of pests'! At last there seemed some small hope for their future and now the hedgehog enjoys full protection in some Continental countries, though not in Britain.

Professor Oken was one of the first to extol the virtues of hedgehogs to a scientific adult readership, but for thousands of years there have been storytellers who have portrayed them in a pleasant light. Even before the Romans, Aesop in ancient Greece, telling his fables to save his own life, showed in 'The Stag and the Hedgehog' how the short-legged hedgehog could beat the magnificent stag, all because Mrs Hedgehog looked identical to her spouse and could be at the finish of the race even before the two competitors had set off. Hedgehogs, it was suggested, were thinking animals. To follow this 'The Fox and the Hedgehog' showed the hedgehog offering assistance to the fox – a good Samaritan.

The German storytellers, the Brothers Grimm, came up with their own version of 'The Stag and the Hedgehog'. Their tale had the hedgehog out-thinking another swift and handsome animal, the hare.

Gradually, in fiction if not in fact, a positive attitude to hedgehogs was taking hold. More than a century ago in *Alice in Wonderland* Lewis Carroll described hedgehogs being used by the Queen of Hearts and Alice as croquet balls until they managed to escape. The twentieth-century hedgehog killed by Ian Campbell of Herne Bay in February 1986 had no such escape. Mr Campbell found the hedgehog rummaging in his dustbin, hit the animal with a broom handle and, when it rolled up to protect itself, he used it as a golf ball. He also said that he regarded the hedgehog as 'vermin'. The hedgehog died from its injuries but Mr Campbell was acquitted of a cruelty prosecution because hedgehogs in the wild are not protected by the 1911 Protection of Animals Act. How can a country renowned as a nation of animal lovers still allow such practices to go unpunished?

It seems unlikely that Mr Campbell had read Beatrix Potter's children's stories when he was young. Anyone who has read *The Tale of Mrs Tiggy-winkle* cannot help but feel warmly towards the little washer-woman forever busy helping other animals with their laundry. All fuss, whiskers and petticoat, Mrs Tiggy-winkle has done more to familiarise both young and old with hedgehogs than any other character in fact or fiction, and I am convinced that we can thank Beatrix Potter for saving the hedgehog for the present generation to see and enjoy.

Since the publication of *Mrs Tiggy-winkle* early this century the hedgehog has become more and more part of all our lives. Even during the 1939–45

Beatrix Potter's Mrs Tiggy-winkle.

Many European countries have featured hedgehogs on their stamps and postmarks.

war HMS *Urchin*, whose badge includes a 'hedgehog proper', was a reminder of the small animal with which nobody had time to bother – except, that is, those in Anderson air-raid shelters who found themselves sharing accommodation with our prickly friends. HMS *Urchin* proudly blazoned her name in battles from Anzio to Okinawa, one of the few places in Asia without its resident hedgehog. HMS *Urchin* may also have carried, like other Royal Navy ships, the newly developed Hedgehog Projector which fired a pattern of anti-submarine mortars more effectively than the traditional depth charges.

The Germans, traditionally fond of their hedgehogs, used a system known as Hedgehog Defence, wherein a central town was protected by outlying strong points. It's easy to see how the system got its name; eventually, though, the Russian army learned to overcome its hedgehog invincibility by merely going around it.

When the war was over and life began to return to normal, the people of Europe, who had lived with desolation for so long, seemed to start taking a new look at the natural world about them, noticing birds, animals and plants as part of their existence not just as exploitable items. The countryside became a consuming topic of conversation. The countries which had suffered the most depredation came forward to lead the world into a new age. The insignificant hedgehog became one of the banners of the new caring societies when it first appeared on the 1953 colourful stamp issues of war-battered Hungary. As the stamps went out around the world, the people of Berlin followed suit, using hedgehog images on their postmarks. Yugoslavia included a hedgehog on its series of forest mammals issued in 1960 and more Eastern Bloc countries followed soon afterwards. The German Democratic Republic launched a Fauna Protection Campaign in 1963; there were no large animals on these stamps, only a beetle, turtle, salamander, toad and, of course, a hedgehog – creatures which had been so often overlooked. Bulgaria also brought out a hedgehog stamp in 1963 and even Albania issued its Forest Animals series the following year.

There were so many letters with hedgehogs on from Eastern Europe that soon Western countries joined the campaign. Switzerland used the hedgehog

to launch its children's fund 'Pro Juventute 1965', with the Netherlands doing the same in 1967, although they did mistake their hedgehog for a porcupine. Africa had its own hedgehog, giving Tunisia reason to include *'l'hérisson'* on its 1968 Fauna series. The Netherlands once again, in 1976, used hedgehogs for its charity stamps until at last the United Kingdom brought out its superb multi-coloured set of wildlife stamps on 5th October 1977.

With all this exposure our hedgehog, so maligned for centuries, was gaining a popular image, becoming a symbol of all that was fine in the countryside. 'Operation Spikey' was the campaign of the Keep Britain Tidy Group which had a massive response from the public in keeping the country clean. The Mammal Society, involved in seeking fresh knowledge about animals, adopted the hedgehog coupled with a pair of binoculars for its logo, as did the Northamptonshire Trust for Nature Conservation which went one better and arranged for Carlsberg, the Danish lager company, to swamp public houses with beer mats emblazoned with our prickly hero. There were hedgehog images everywhere; companies all round the world used it on their letter headings.

Even the British began to care about hedgehogs. The Henry Doubleday Research Association advocated gardens free of chemicals and slug pellets. Major Adrian Coles spotted a hedgehog trapped in a cattle grid and designed and advocated an escape ramp. Hedgehogabilia became the craze – stone ones, glass ones, cuddly ones, hedgehog pictures and even mechanical hedgehogs were suddenly on display everywhere. The Age of the Hedgehog was dawning.

Simultaneously the new communication marvel of television had been creeping into our living rooms.

A selection of 'hedgehogabilia' collected by Claudia Perry (photo Mike Harlow).

Those inanimate illustrations of wild animals and birds which had been our only contact with wildlife were suddenly brought to life. Pioneer explorers like Armand and Michaela Denis and David Attenborough, armed only with film cameras, hunted exotic creatures all round the world. The public clamoured for more; at last we were able to see film of Britain's own wildlife which had remained for so long unseen on our own doorstep. We experienced the untameable freedom of the wild cat; the mastery of the fox caught by light-intensive photography; the innermost secrets of a badger sett;

and, on one memorable evening, a whole half hour devoted to hedgehogs. It was marvellous wildlife photography but even the BBC could not resist those old stories, and 'The Great Hedgehog Mystery' devoted film time to the 'apples on the spine' myth and the hedgehog's cow-suckling reputation.

The caring hedgehog of Aesop's 'The Fox and the Hedgehog' has surfaced again as Herby, the mascot of the Hertfordshire Hospice Care Service; and we can now enjoy Hedgehog Crisps, which do not of course use hedgehogs to flavour them but only organically grown ingredients. Philip Lewis who runs

Hedgehog Foods is firmly committed to the welfare of hedgehogs and consistently gives support to all our projects involving hedgehog conservation.

When we opened the world's first hedgehog hospital, St Tiggywinkles, we found that 'pricklies' were people's favourite form of wildlife. People saw hedgehogs, knew hedgehogs and more than anything wanted them to be protected and looked after. They are inoffensive, useful little creatures and because of the persecution we heaped upon their ancestors we owe them this protection.

Hedgehog Crisps' logo

Spikey says-
Please take your litter home

The logo of the Keep Britain Tidy Group.

The Beast Itself

In spite of its small size and apparent vulnerability the hedgehog, with many of its insectivore cousins, has managed to outlast many giant species of both reptile and mammal, having survived more or less unchanged since the early pioneering days when mammals first challenged the reptiles for dominance of the earth.

At the end of the Permian geological era, 225 million years ago, the earth consisted of one gigantic land mass surrounded by an enormous, hostile sea populated by all kinds of weird and wonderful monsters. Amphibians, reptiles and insects walked this vast continent, but at the same time there were the first stirrings of mammal evolution.

All previous life had been cold-blooded (ectothermic), relying on the sun and shade to warm it up or cool it down. Reptiles were unable to feed until the sun's rays had warmed them and as they all became active at the same time it was inevitable that confrontations for food ensued. The larger reptiles found they could retain heat for much longer, giving them a distinct advantage over their smaller relatives. In the ensuing Triassic era of 35 million years the larger reptiles thrived and began to evolve into even larger animals. Growing to enormous size, they dwarfed their predecessors – this was the dawn of the dinosaur dynasty.

These gigantic animals needed to exploit all available food sources to support their prodigious metabolism and, as most of them were at this stage vegetarians, the smaller reptiles had to turn to an alternative supply of food and find a method of heat retention that would enable them to compete with the dinosaurs.

There were at this time innumerable species of insects which were an available source of food for many of the smaller species, but the insects too were ectothermic and at their warmest and most elusive just when the reptiles were active. The larger animals could not survive on this minute and evasive diet so the smaller animals had no competition for this food source, but had to find an easier way of capturing it.

If they could feed at night or in the cool periods of the day, not only would they find many of the insects sluggish or inactive but they would avoid encounters with the larger carnivorous reptiles which were gradually evolving. As no outside heat source was available during these periods the reptiles, to survive, had to generate their own body heat from within. They became the first warm-blooded animals, the first mammals.

These earliest mammals kept themselves very small and unobtrusive. Most were the size of the

'How many more tragic deaths before we perfect the tyre-piercing quill?'

present day shrews with a very similar lifestyle, scurrying beneath any available cover. The dinosaurs continued to evolve and, in the ensuing millennia when much of Britain was covered by a warm shallow sea populated with gigantic ichthyosaurs and plesiosaurs, they even took to flying, growing feathers to keep warm and, most ominous of all for the new mammals, started to generate their own body heat. These first birds were meat-eaters and no doubt were a threat to the small mammals who now had greater incentive for nocturnal feeding to avoid being preyed upon.

The Triassic turned through the Jurassic era into the Cretaceous, seeing the dinosaurs, birds and mammals increase their strength and variety. However, the many forms of dinosaur found it hard to adapt to the increasingly seasonal climate and with the new type of mammal competing more successfully for the available food they started to falter and, all of a sudden, 64 million years ago the dinosaurs died out, leaving only the birds as a reminder of their 160 million year dynasty.

Now the stage was free for the mammals to grow and prosper. During the Cretaceous era they had split into two groups: the marsupials which gave birth to embryonic youngsters having a precarious upbringing in their mother's pouch, and the placental mammals which carried their young inside the body attached to a placenta. The marsupials have survived only in Australia – where there were no predators or placental mammals to compete with them – and as opossums in the Americas. On the other hand, the placental mammals continued to thrive, eventually evolving into the different species of mammal which exist today and which include man.

Some of the early insectivorous mammals

branched out to form more sophisticated species of animals while the remainder continued with very little change up to the present day. The first hedgehogs started to appear in the Oligocene period about 30 million years ago. They did not have spines but they were identical to the present day hairy hedgehogs, the moon rats, of Asia. The five genera still hanging onto existence are probably the most primitive of all the placental mammals and definitely have the oldest family tree.

The Miocene period which followed saw the dawn of the hedgehog invasion: by the end of the period, about 5 million years ago, the hedgehogs had occupied every corner of the world, with the exception of isolated Australia, South America, Madagascar and, of course, Antarctica. Fossil hedgehogs have been found in North America but for some reason the species did not succeed there, whereas in all the other occupied territories they have thrived with very little change.

At this time, between 4 and 5 million years ago, as more mammal species than ever before or since spread across the world it was fashionable to grow very large. The hedgehog family had its own big brother which grew to about the size of the present day badger. A giant hairy hedgehog, *Deinogalerix*, lived in Italy and, as the Mediterranean was then dry, it had probably spread further south into North Africa which was much closer to Europe than it is now. Its fossil remains have been found in a late Miocene excavation at Gargano in southern Italy. Knowing a hedgehog's penchant for food larger than itself, I imagine that *Deinogalerix* must have been a formidable creature, no doubt eating other mammals as well as masses of insects in order to satisfy that enormous appetite. It had the distinction of being the largest known insectivore but, like the

bulky dinosaurs, it too went into decline and eventual extinction, leaving the moon rat as the largest of the insectivores remaining today.

Over the last 5 million years hedgehogs have continued to prosper, adopting the familiar spiny pelage or coat to combat the threat of the new smaller lethal predators which began to appear. The fearsome-looking sabre-toothed tiger, the smilodon, was not, despite its fearsome looks, a very successful predator, and soon died out, but its relatives, the smaller biting cats, without those outsize canine teeth, were extremely efficient killers, paving the way for the present day lions and tigers. There were also new species of predators, dogs and bears, but somehow the hedgehogs and their insectivore cousins have managed to survive.

We know for certain that hedgehogs were firmly established in Britain by the middle Pleistocene period about 2 million years ago. Many fossilised bones have been unearthed recently in East Anglia but as spines, being modified hairs, do not fossilise very well, there is no evidence of these.

Even 2 million years ago, when the earth had settled and all the gargantuan ancestors of some of the world's animals had ceased to be, the hedgehogs of Europe still had other catastrophes to face. Before long most of Britain and Europe was covered with an enormous sheet of ice, the Ice Age was beginning. While Britain was still joined to the Continent the hedgehogs which survived the increasingly cold winters could gradually move south to milder climates where they could safely hibernate through the cold spells. Coming back during the warmer inter-glacial periods they could not re-establish themselves until finally the ice sheet receded completely. As the ice melted so the level of the sea rose, leaving Britain and Ireland cut off from Europe. Any animals which had not crossed into Britain could not now do so, hence the more varied fauna on the Continent. As it was, only one of the insectivores, the pygmy shrew, had made it as far as Ireland but mainland Britain now had the mole resident, as well as three species of shrew and the hedgehog. Only later were hedgehogs introduced to Ireland – probably as food. The climate was now too warm for the mammoths, woolly rhinoceroses, bison, bears and arctic foxes, which all died out, having no escape route back to the Continent. Still the insectivores thrived, but there was a new threat to their survival, one which also followed the retreating ice cap into Britain. This was early man whose descendants have such an important role to play in preserving remnants of those early primitive days.

The European hedgehog *Erinaceus europaeus* was now established over most of western Europe from the coast of the Mediterranean Sea north to Finland and central Sweden and eastwards across northern Russia into western Siberia and had by this time developed its spiny protective coat. Its very close relative, or some say merely a sub-species, *Erinaceus concolor*, which was also spiny, filled the hedgehog niche in eastern Europe, meeting *Erinaceus europaeus* along a line roughly drawn between the Baltic Sea and the Adriatic Sea. They overlap and, no doubt, have interbred along a 200 kilometre strip of Czechoslovakia. *Erinaceus concolor* has even extended its range into the Middle East where it shares its territory with the spiny long-eared hedgehog, *Hemiechinus auritus*.

Nobody will ever know just how many hedgehog species there have been. It is rare enough for any animal's remains to become fossilised and even more unusual for anybody to find those fossils. Even now there is no definite agreement on how many species

Early nineteenth-century engraving of 'The Hedge Hog'. Fig.1 without bristles.

still remain in existence. It is generally accepted that there are only five species of hairy hedgehogs (moon rats) remaining and as these belong to five separate families it is not hard to imagine that many species have been lost forever. Perhaps as these are the direct descendants of the first mammals their line of evolution is about to come to an end. It is a pity that man seems to be helping them on their way to oblivion.

Their slightly more advanced cousins, the spined hedgehogs, are more secure for the time being, but nobody seems to agree on just how many species there are. Some authors suggest only twelve species, while Konrad Herter's renowned monograph, entitled simply *Hedgehogs*, detailed over twenty species and sub-species. Currently it seems to be accepted that there are eleven species of spined hedgehogs. They are indigenous to the continents of Europe, Asia and Africa, whereas those in New Zealand were introduced for acclimatisation experiments in the nineteenth century.

Both the hairy hedgehogs and the spined species have similar anatomies and metabolisms, any distinctive differences being in their external appearance. To qualify as a member of the *Erinaceidae* an animal must possess the typically hedgehog pattern of 36 teeth I had recognised in my first hedgehog casualty. Often it was only a few teeth and fragments of jaw that enabled palaeontologists to identify and classify early insectivore fossils. Having changed very little since the Miocene era an insectivore's teeth are small and numerous – some species having 44 teeth, the maximum for any placental mammal.

Any mammal's teeth, including those of hedgehogs, are always in the same order, although in varying combination. At the front of the jaw are the incisors, specialised in the hedgehog but quite insignificant in most other predatory mammals. Behind these are the canine teeth used so effectively by the cats and other carnivores. The pre-molars and molars make up the complement of teeth being used for the grinding or chewing of food. Each side of the jaw is a mirror image of the other. As each family of animals has a specific combination of teeth a quick investigation of just one side is a sound method of identification.

Unfortunately, bearing in mind my experience on the golf course, the only way one can usually study the teeth pattern of a wild animal is in an exposed skull. However, notice how the skull is short and blunt although hedgehogs have typically insectivoral pointed snouts. The soft overhang which protrudes over the bottom jaw allows for great mobility in the snout and as the nostrils open to the side the hedgehog is able to root around in soil and leaf litter without blocking its nasal passages. More primitive than other insectivores, the hedgehog's skull however possesses fully formed robust zygomatic arches (cheekbones) just below and protecting the eye sockets. These arches are completely missing in shrews and are weakly formed in moles and even *Deinogalerix*, the giant prehistoric hairy hedgehog, had none to speak of.

A full grown European hedgehog usually has a skull measuring 54 millimetres to 64 millimetres long by 39 millimetres wide although it has been said that the Thracian variety from Macedonia is somewhat larger. More robust than that of other insectivores, the skull protects a very simple brain devoid of all ridges apparent in the brain of higher mammals, although the area of the sense of smell, the olfactory lobes, are well developed, enabling the hedgehog to detect prey, even underground, with that long constantly damp nose. Hedgehogs nearly always have runny noses but they do not have colds: the moisture greatly enhances their sense of smell, particularly useful to them since their eyes are not very efficient.

They do not have 'hedge-piggy' little eyes but

The hedgehog skull – note the long incisors and small canine teeth.

quite large, very dark brown to black eyes that protrude slightly, as bright as buttons. Like most non-primitive mammals they do not have the ability to perceive colour but they may take notice of something yellow. The hedgehog's hearing is not finely tuned to high-frequency sounds like that of rats or bats but is more in line with our own hearing capabilities. A bat's ears can pick up sounds with frequencies of over 100 kilohertz while a human can only register up to 20 kilohertz. Hedgehogs can detect frequencies of about 45 kilohertz, perfectly adequate for detecting any strange sound that may mean danger or for picking up the munching of an unwary caterpillar or the rustling of a beetle in leaf litter.

Even when it is relaxed and unrolled the European hedgehog's ears are not very noticeable but its cousins, the desert hedgehogs and, aptly named, long-eared hedgehogs, have made use of their exaggerated ears to help dispel the heat of their native hot, dry desert and scrubland. In the hotter, dry parts of the world where they live, there is little vegetation or leaf litter so the desert and long-eared

hedgehogs use their long legs to scurry over the ground picking up food as they go. There are no trees with exposed roots to provide nest sites so the hedgehogs have learned to dig short burrows in which to avoid the heat of the day. Surprisingly enough, under that plump body, our European hedgehog has fairly long legs and can turn a good burst of speed when necessary, although not quite up to the 40 mph one bus driver claimed to have paced. A hedgehog has been timed, hopefully not over a measured mile, at 6.5 feet (2 metres) per second, the equivalent of approximately 4.5 miles an hour. It would probably take 13.5 minutes to run the mile.

Having long legs also enables the hedgehog to perform all manner of contortions in order to scratch between the spines on its back. It is often said that it is because hedgehogs cannot groom that they

Mobile hip joints and long claws enable the hedgehog to groom itself.

45

suffer from masses of skin parasites, but you have only to watch a hedgehog leaving its nest in the evening to see how it manages to manoeuvre each of its hind legs practically out of their joints, reaching right over its back. The skin on its back is remarkably thick and insensitive: the hedgehog is probably unaware of most of its parasite load.

Its sense of touch seems to be concentrated around the face and in the long guard hairs fringing the spiny back. When inspecting a hedgehog for injuries, one false move to touch the face or fringe of hair causes it to bring forward its head spines and immediately roll up into a ball.

The hairs along its sides and underneath are fairly soft and range in colour from dark brown to very pale, almost white. These are not unusual in a mammal; it is the modified hairs, the spines, which are so characteristic of hedgehogs. Its first full set of brown spines are complete when it is about three weeks old. From then on it continues to grow extra spines as its body size increases. Some large individuals have as many as 7000 spines. Hedgehogs would be completely defenceless if they moulted the majority of their spines annually, as other animals moult hair, so they replace them one at a time at irregular intervals, some spines lasting for over two years.

The spine itself is a masterpiece of natural engineering. Being only about an inch in length it is made up of a number of vertical transparent tubes rather like a roll of corrugated cardboard, giving it the appearance of being ribbed. The inherent strength of this form of construction allows the spine to bend without kinking. Dr Vincent of Reading University found that hedgehog spines, being 25 times longer than they are wide, gave the optimum elasticity: a hedgehog relies on its spines to absorb the shock of

The hedgehog spine is generally shaded white to brown but pure white albinos are not uncommon.

a fall or collision – if the spines were any shorter, the shock would pass on to the hedgehog and, if they were any longer, the spines could well become permanently kinked. Where the spine grows out of the body it has a slightly curved neck terminating in a small bulbous end. The curved neck further helps absorb any shock while the bulbous end prevents the spine being driven into the body. Incredibly strong, the bulbous end is so well designed that it is possible to pick up even the largest hedgehog by a single spine. It is possible, too, that the spine with its hollow interior has another property: it may well act as insulation, particularly when hedgehogs are out on colder nights. But the main advantage of growing all those spines is to protect the hedgehog from the smaller predators such as the stoat and weasel, and the larger birds of prey.

Each of the spines is attached by its own muscle to an enormous sheet of muscle, the *panniculus carnosus*, that lines the back of the hedgehog. As the animal starts to roll up, first the head and rump are pulled down and inwards then the *panniculus carnosus* comes into play folding the hedgehog inside it. An even stronger muscle, the *musculus orbicularis*, which acts as a purse string to the *panniculus*, then tightens

A family goes foraging.

until every soft part of the hedgehog is safely tucked away and 'sealed in the bag'. As the *panniculus* contracts it activates each muscle attached to the spines which are then flexed erect and pointing in different directions, forming a barrage of spines clustered in small star-shaped groups.

Catching a hedgehog in an unguarded moment is virtually impossible but, if you should manage to do so, look at its underside which, covered in long brown hair, is more like what we would expect of any other mammal. However, certain typical hedgehog characteristics are immediately apparent: there are two rows of five nipples but they are along the outer edges of the body, presumably to allow prickly babies to suckle without causing too much discomfort to the females. It's now possible to sex the hedgehog: the male has its penis positioned roughly in the centre of its stomach but its testes are carried inside the body and are not visible. The female's genitals are situated directly in front of its anal opening. The male hedgehog has the largest reproductive tract, in proportion to its body size, of any mammal, often taking up as much as 10 per cent of its body weight. When they are mating the female lays its spines flat and pushes out its soft-haired rear end beyond the spines so that the male's disproportionately long penis can easily penetrate. In very young hedgehogs both sexes look identical but over a period of weeks the male's external genitals migrate to their position in the centre of the body.

It's also now possible to look at the hedgehog's typically insectivore feet, which have five toes on each foot in contrast to the similarly sized rodents with only four on each of their front feet. However, there is a hedgehog, *Erinaceus albiventris* of Africa, which is usually called the four-toed hedgehog because some of this sub-species do not have the great toe on their hind feet.

Each toe, especially on the hind feet, ends in a

47

very long claw. The claws on the hind feet are exceptionally long on the middle three toes – useful for grooming – while those on the front feet can be used for digging either for insects or under sheds and logs for nest sites.

One last feature usually only seen when the hedgehog is unrolled is the short tail. This has no spines, being covered by sparse hairs, and it can be tucked in and out of the way when the animal rolls up.

Internally, the hedgehog is, as my vet put it as he operated to remedy a hernia after a road accident, 'just like the inside of a dog or cat'. The original physiology of the early hedgehogs seems to have been retained and adopted in more sophisticated forms by most other meat-eating mammals. Admittedly its backbone is more flexible than most, enabling it to curl up into that impregnable ball. Other special characteristics of the hedgehog skeletal frame include the fusing of the radius and ulna near the elbow joint and the tibia and fibula near the ankles.

Of course hedgehogs vary in weight and size. *Erinaceus europaeus* in Britain weighs in at about 700 grams after its first year, growing to an average of just over 1 kilogram, although some older animals may weigh around 2 kilograms. Of course just before hibernation, with plenty of fat on board, a hedgehog will be heavier than normal, but after having lost almost a third of its weight through hibernation it will be much lighter in the early part of the year.

Its size is very flexible. A wary hedgehog ready to curl up may be only 19 or 20 centimetres long, but the same hedgehog when running or scavenging may stretch out to 23 to 25 centimetres. As they get older they tend to put centimetres on their girth

'He's been terribly withdrawn recently.'

rather than their length, but the horrifying statistics are now suggesting that hedgehogs are not getting old. A hedgehog used to be thought of as living for up to ten years, with one third of that spent in hibernation. In view of all the new hazards it has been frequently suggested that the average hedgehog expectation of life is now little more than two years. I sincerely hope that conservation movements and methods of organic pest control will help to improve that situation, as animals having less than two years' life expectancy cannot maintain the species.

Take note of your hedgehogs. All over the world they can be heard at night going about their business of snuffling along at ground level, sniffing and listening for caterpillars, beetles, grubs and slugs, in fact anything that vaguely resembles meat. Listen to them lip-smacking and obviously relishing their food in temperate Europe, the hot dry deserts of Asia and Africa or up in the tropical mountains of south-east Asia. Apart from moon rats which are hairy, they all look much the same, although some are prettier than others, some have large ears and their spines vary dramatically in colour.

Marie Baguena

Spiky Creatures Around the World

FIRST OF all, let's dispense with all those creatures which have adopted a coat of spines but have no connection at all with true hedgehogs. Found in all walks of the animal world, look-alikes include spiny sea urchins, called after the old name for hedgehogs, spiky eels, prickly caterpillars and, most confusing of all the spined mammals, land animals with four legs and the typical head-down habits of the true hedgehog. Sometimes even an orphaned baby hedgehog will make a mistake and adopt an old scrubbing brush as a comforting mother substitute.

However, a closer look at the impostors will show that some are rodents, and others are monotremes – like the spiny anteater or echidna. A porcupine has spines, or should I say quills, that present a prickly creature but here the similarity ends. Firstly, porcupines are true rodents with two pairs of constantly growing incisor teeth that are typical of the more familiar rodents – rabbits, rats, squirrels and, one of the porcupine's closest relatives, the guinea pig. Porcupines regularly climb trees whereas a hedgehog will rarely attempt to scale even the most gently sloping of trunks. Porcupines are, in the main, vegetarians living on a diet of berries, fruit, bulbs, roots and, when it suits them, cultivated crops like potatoes, maize and ground nuts. They are found on all five continents and unlike hedgehogs they can be spotted in most parts of North and South America. If you hear somebody from America talk about their hedgehogs, you can be sure that they are referring to porcupines or ground hogs, which are the prolific ground squirrels (*Marmota monax*) living deep in burrows on the open plains. There are also species of porcupine in other parts of the world, including Central Africa and many parts of southern Asia.

A porcupine should not be approached; it will not hesitate, if it feels threatened, to use its needle-sharp quills as weapons of defence. Take heed if it starts rattling its quills and stamping its feet: it may well run backwards into you, leaving some of those quills broken off in your legs. Try not to take a close look at a porcupine quill, but if you should find one, notice how it is straight and pointed at both ends unlike the hedgehog's which has that shock-absorber modification close to the body.

The echidna of Australia and New Guinea is a much more docile animal preferring to bury itself if threatened. Often referred to as the Australian hedgehog, the echidna is one of the world's most remarkable animals but it is not a hedgehog. It is not even a marsupial, the line of mammals which evolved alongside the insectivores, hedgehogs and other placentals; it is in fact a monotreme – an egg-laying mammal – of which only three species, two echidnas and the platypus, have survived. Echidnas are much larger than hedgehogs, weighing up to 10 kilograms and growing up to 1 metre in length, and the long-beaked echidna has very few spines.

You should now be able to tell one of the hedgehog species from most of the look-alikes, but the tenrecs of Madagascar, now the Malagasy Republic, need more than a cursory glance to identify them. They have evolved in their own way ever since the island of Madagascar split from the main African continent soon after the first insectivores had started to prosper in the Palaeocene era, 60 million years ago. Somehow, by convergent evolution, three species have developed spines just like those of the hedgehog, with the greater hedgehog tenrec (*Setifer setosus*) being the most similar in size, build and habit. It can roll into a ball, though not quite as securely as the true hedgehogs, but will abandon that form of defence and advance on an aggressor, hissing with its mouth open and head-bucking, quite unlike our own placid hedgehog. When its mouth is open, it is possible to see that it does not possess the prominent incisor teeth of true hedgehogs but has the full canines of other insectivores such as the mole. As it

It looks like a hedgehog but it's the lesser hedgehog tenrec (photographed by Tom Cooper at Jersey Wildlife Preservation Trust)

walks, its hind feet point out at right-angles to its body, evidence that it is not a hedgehog.

Its much smaller cousin, the lesser or pygmy hedgehog tenrec (*Echinops telfairi*), is a miniature replica of *Setifer* being only a few centimetres long. It is too small to be a true hedgehog, and it has only 32 teeth instead of the necessary 36.

If you look at a young common tenrec (*Tenrec ecaudatus*), you would think it was a baby hedgehog. It has dark and light spines just like a hedgehog but as it grows, so its covering of spines is overtaken by bristles and coarse hairs; those that remain can still be very effective as a deterrent in a head-bucking attack. At about 38 centimetres in length and with a powerful bite, it can be a nasty animal to encounter, quite unhedgehog-like.

The true hedgehogs are not normally aggressive, often resorting only to a snake-like hiss, but my experience has shown that there are individual characters which will not hesitate to bite if handled. However, due to the nature of their teeth and small canines, they will very seldom break the skin.

Around the world there are true indigenous hedgehogs in Europe, Africa, Asia and there is the introduced European hedgehog in New Zealand. There is constant debate on just how many species of spiny hedgehogs there are. Knowing the colour variations seen in British hedgehogs, it seems fool-hardy to try to designate every colour change as a separate species. As far as I can establish, there are eleven distinct species of the spiny hedgehog and five species of hairy hedgehog (the moon rats).

They all belong to the family of *Erinaceidae*, which is divided into two sub-families: the *Erinaceinae* are the spiny hedgehogs, while the *Echinosoricinae* are the moon rats. There are three genera of spiny hedgehog: *Erinaceus*, which includes all the Euro-

pean hedgehogs, *Hemiechinus*, the long-eared hedge-hogs; and *Paraechinus*, the desert hedgehogs. The five species of moon rat belong to five separate genera which suggests that there were originally far more species which have since died out.

The most familiar of the *Erinaceus* is the Western hedgehog, *Erinaceus europaeus*, which has been for so long a familiar part of the European daily life, giving its name to many other familiar items like hedgehog broom (*Erinacea pungens*), the hedgehog cactus (*Echinocactus grussonii*) and even a toadstool, the wood hedgehog or urchin of the woods (*Hydnum repandum*) which is apparently very tasty when young.

Like other animals which adopt a low profile under hedgerows, in woodland and on grassland, the Western hedgehog is overall a dull brown nondescript colour with only its black shiny nose and dark button eyes breaking the camouflage. Its coat of spines seems to blend perfectly with its background, but a close inspection shows that each spine is mainly white with a deep-brown band, that may be almost black, around the centre. Apart from very young hedgehogs, which may still retain some of their baby-white spines, there are some adults with a smattering of white ones, particularly in southern

Western hedgehog, Erinaceus europaeus.

Spain where generally *Erinaceus europaeus* tends to be of a much lighter colour than in other parts of Europe. Wholly albino hedgehogs with pink eyes and completely white spines do occur infrequently but, as with all albino animals, they tend to be too weak and conspicuous to survive in the wild. Varying degrees of partial albinism do occur and thrive, in particular those hedgehogs which have a pink nose instead of the usual black one.

The part of the hedgehog so rarely seen, its underbelly, is covered with coarse brown hair varying in shade from white to the much darker colour that is a feature of the Irish hedgehogs which have prospered there since they were introduced originally as a source of food. Where the Western hedgehog meets its first cousin *Erinaceus concolor*, the Eastern hedgehog which has a distinct white breast, there are hybrids with varying degrees of white breast markings.

Both species of European hedgehog are similar in most other respects, adopting an identical lifestyle and foraging by night under hedgerows, or over pasture land and on the edges of woodland. However, recently they have come to rely on the insects and grubs that proliferate around the towns and their gardens. In London hedgehogs have now been recorded in every borough, and in Berlin they are very common although this high population probably results from their introduction in the 1930s by city dwellers keeping them as pets in their gardens.

Hedgehogs like to be comfortable when sleeping. They prefer their nests to be dry especially during hibernation. They will only nest in an area where there is plenty of nest material, preferably in the deciduous woodlands or large gardens where the fallen leaves serve not only as nest material but also as good hunting grounds rich with grubs and insects.

For these reasons they will not move into the bland conifer forests which have become a feature of Britain's countryside nor will they choose to live in marshy areas or damp woods, although quite a few perish in winter floods if they have not picked a dry enough nesting site.

Before hibernation, hedgehogs need to feed well and build up enough fat reserves to last through the colder months. Even then, many do not make the transition into spring and at the northern limit of their range an extra-long winter can mean disaster to local populations. Although Finnish hedgehogs are said to be more tolerant of extreme conditions, in general hedgehogs are not found in areas where the winters are particularly harsh. None are found north of 63° latitude in Europe and in mountainous areas they generally keep below the tree line, being found up to 2800 metres high in the Caucasus mountains, only up to 1800 metres in the Alps and as low as 400 metres in the cold and damp highlands of Scotland and Wales. The far northern areas of Europe, Iceland and northern Finland are too extreme for hedgehogs and even in Norway the Western hedgehog is thin on the ground. Mrs Naess, who seems to be the only person taking in injured hedgehogs in Norway, suggests that they are in sharp decline and should be classed as an endangered species.

Caring for hedgehogs in Sweden is Yvonne Gustafsson who takes in wildlife casualties, making regular calls to injured eagles, goshawks, and harriers, but still devoting much of her time to the less glamorous hedgehog. Being slightly further south than Norway and having a far more hospitable terrain seems to suit the Swedish hedgehogs which appear to be thriving. Keeping well clear of the frozen north, the Western hedgehog has colonised some of northern Russia and western Siberia as far as the Irtysh River.

Parts of Britain are above the 60° parallel and do not have indigenous populations of hedgehogs, but hedgehogs have been deliberately introduced to a few northern islands. On some islands, the hedgehog is said to be barely surviving, while on others – in particular North Ronaldsay in the Orkneys – there is reputed to be a population explosion. The hedgehogs which were introduced to Alderney have proved a welcome addition to the wildlife of the small island. Oddly, there have been two distinct colour variations among Alderney hedgehogs, one dark and the other quite pale: possibly some Spanish hedgehogs were shipped in as well as the normal British version.

Hedgehogs have also been introduced to non-British islands in the North Sea, in particular the Friesian Islands. These are very low-lying and need artificial sea walls to make the farmland practical for agriculture. Many tons of bundles of faggots for building sea walls were shipped from the mainland of Europe together with stowaway hedgehogs which were using the bundles as nests and hibernacula.

In 1927 an artificial causeway was constructed to make the carriage of materials to the island of Sylt much easier. Apparently the burrowing of immigrant water voles threatened to undermine the causeway and so, for some reason (although they do not prey on water voles), three hedgehogs were brought over from Schleswig Holstein to combat the menace. Nobody appears to know the outcome of this experiment, but hedgehogs are now firmly established as part of the Sylt fauna.

Irresponsibility seemed to be the motto for animal introductions but despite this the Western hedgehog is now thriving in New Zealand where, before their introduction in the nineteenth century, there were no insectivore mammals, only large numbers of flightless insectivore birds, in particular the near mammal kiwi. Hedgehogs were introduced to South Island for acclimatisation experiments in 1870, 1885 and 1892, apparently without account being taken of the possible effects on New Zealand's renowned population of flightless avifauna. Luckily the hedgehogs appear to have fitted in with little detrimental effect on the ground-nesting birds. In 1910 some of the South Island's hedgehogs were transferred to the North Island where they have also established themselves in the milder climate and a terrain not too dissimilar from that of Europe. Both populations of hedgehog have adapted well, even changing their breeding pattern to the period of November to March and taking their hibernation between July and October, although in milder areas some hedgehogs have dispensed with the need for a long winter sleep. Taking advantage of the shorter winters and longer summers the hedgehogs have extended their breeding period and, consequently, populations are higher than in the home country, Britain.

The one great difference between the New Zealand and European hedgehog is that the former does not suffer from the hedgehog flea, *Archaeopsylla erinacei*. This is not a twist of evolution – I would assume that the Victorian scientists who shipped the animals across the world probably removed any fleas before they left Europe. However, there have been a few records of New Zealand hedgehogs picking up local fleas and they seem to suffer more than British animals from heavy mite infestations.

There are only minor differences between the Western hedgehog and its counterpart *Erinaceus concolor* or *roumanicus*, the Eastern hedgehog. The Eastern hedgehog has a noticeably smart white bib

Eastern hedgehog, Erinaceus concolor.

transcaucasicus around the area but without any reference to a difference in size.

The other hedgehog of Europe is of a quite different appearance to the previous *Erinacei*. This, the Algerian or vagrant hedgehog, *Erinaceus algirus*, is slightly smaller than its European cousins, weighing only up to 850 grams. It is much paler in colour with a totally white underside; only the southern Spanish variety of the Western hedgehog is lighter but the Algerian hedgehog is easily identified by the pencil-wide parting in the spines on its head and its longer legs and larger ears. It walks much higher on its legs, and does not need to hibernate in its native North Africa, although those which have been introduced to the eastern coastal strip of Spain and the south of France will hibernate in severe winters. This is the hedgehog of the packaged holiday resorts, the hedgehog resident on Majorca, Minorca, Malta, Ibiza, Formentera and sadly the one often seen squashed on the road to the airport above Lanzarote in the Canary Islands. In its native North Africa the Algerian hedgehog has colonised the whole northern fringe from Morocco to Cyrenaica including, of course, Algeria, Tunisia and Libya. Its limits to the

extending from its chin to halfway down its chest but the other difference, in the skulls of the two species, can only be seen *post mortem* by dividing the length of the top jaw bone by height to give the maxillary index. The Western hedgehog has an index of one or less while the Eastern hedgehog's is greater than one. Extending eastward from the line between the Baltic and Adriatic the Eastern hedgehog is established in Poland, Czechoslovakia, Hungary, Yugoslavia, Greece and all other eastern European countries including southern Russia down into Turkey, Iran and along the Mediterranean coast into Israel. It is also the resident hedgehog on Crete and many of the Greek islands.

Konrad of Megenberg wrote in the fourteenth century of a large hedgehog which he called *Cirogrillus*. Walter and Christl Podushka, in their book *Dearest Prickles*, thought that *Cirogrillus* might be the giant Thracian hedgehog of which they found three examples in the Yugoslavian part of Macedonia. This is true Eastern hedgehog territory so it seems strange that Herter in his treatise on hedgehogs did not mention the Thracian sub-species although he did mark a small pocket of what he called *Erinaceus*

Algerian hedgehog, Erinaceus algirus.

south are the uncultivated areas on the southern border of the Atlas mountains where its range overlaps with the first of the desert hedgehogs, *Paraechinus aethiopicus.*

In keeping with the hot dry terrain of its native Africa, the Algerian hedgehog feeds largely on grasshoppers and has better table manners than the Western hedgehog, probably because, not having the cover of hedgerows and woodland, it has to be quiet to avoid detection. Its young take longer to develop than the Western hedgehog; it is 22 days before their eyes are open, 44 days before they start to feed themselves and the mother still suckles them until about their fifty-ninth day.

Acute hearing seems to be very important in the hot, dry areas and the desert hedgehog, *Paraechinus aethiopicus,* which lives in the Sahara south of the Algerian hedgehog's range, has much larger ears. Even the bony part of its middle ear has developed into a tympanic bulla that greatly enhances its auditory perception. The desert hedgehog lives in the harshest conditions possible and probably has specialised kidneys to enable it to go without water for considerable lengths of time. Even smaller than its northern cousin, it weighs only between 400 and 700 grams. It has a smaller parting of spines on its head, but the spines have vertical grooves on them – possibly another adaptation to its harsh lifestyle. If there is sand or soil the desert hedgehog will excavate burrows 40 to 50 centimetres deep where it can escape the heat. Where there is no possibility of digging, it will hide up in cracks in rocks or boulders without the comfort of any nest material. It breeds just once a year between July and September and produces up to six young, which it will protect by raising its head spines, screaming and even attacking an aggressor. It's quite a brave little

character, liking nothing better than a meal of scorpion having first bitten off the sting.

Overall the desert hedgehog appears very pale in colour: its forehead, chin, throat, the front of its breast and its ears are white, and it has a dark brown face and tail. Its stomach is spotted brown and white, while its spines are a sandy colour with dark tips. Darker forms and completely white animals are not uncommon.

South of the Sahara, in a broad band from Gambia in the west to Somalia in the east and including Kenya and Tanzania, where so many fossilised hedgehog species have been excavated, lives the four-toed or white-bellied hedgehog, *Erinaceus albiventris.* Similar in size to the European hedgehog, its general colouring is speckled black and white, with white spines banded dark brown. Although it lives in a very warm climate and may need to aestivate – the hot climate equivalent of hibernation – if it becomes too hot, one pair in captivity in Europe were found by Grzimek to hibernate when the ambient temperature dropped to 6°C. The same pair mated similarly to the Western hedgehog followed by a gestation period of between 37 and 38 days. Although there were three litters per year the female

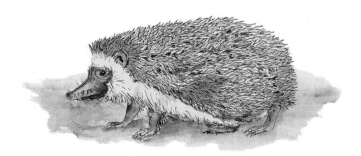

Four-toed or white-bellied hedgehog, Erinaceus albiventris.

Desert hedgehog, Paraechinus aethiopicus, *on a feeding foray.*

always ate the young, a habit I'm afraid to say of captive hedgehogs all over the world.

The ears of *Erinaceus albiventris* are shorter than its spines, as are the Western hedgehog's, but for some reason most of this species of hedgehog lack the great toes on their hind feet. This does not occur in any other species of insectivore, although its near neighbour the desert hedgehog has only a very small great toe.

The four-toed hedgehog likes open country with dry soil and plenty of cover and can also be found in woodlands, bush savannah, thickets and even 1800 metres up Mount Kilimanjaro. Unlike the badger and fox with which the Western hedgehog has to contend, this hedgehog has to resort to hissing and spitting to deter enemies like hyenas, jackals, honey badgers, wild dogs and large owls. Also known as *Erinaceus pruneri*, it takes cover and nests in holes in the ground, between rocks and stones and inside the giant termite hills which are a feature of Central Africa.

The rest of Africa, including south-west Angola, Botswana, Zimbabwe south of the Zambesi, Mozambique and South Africa, is the domain of the Cape hedgehog, *Erinaceus frontalis*. Very similar in build to the four-toed hedgehog it too has white spines, but with a broader dark band, offset by a dark brown muzzle and forehead with a white band that passes over the shoulders onto the throat and chest. Its legs and underside are greyish to dark brown. It has more need to hibernate than the four-toed hedgehog and is quite often asleep or lethargic between May and August.

Preferring a wetter climate than do the other African hedgehogs, it relies on at least 30 centimetres of rain annually. Found on wooded savannahs, woodland, open grassland, fields and small shrubby

Cape hedgehog, Erinaceus frontalis.

kopjes it is also the garden hedgehog of South Africa. It is more nomadic than its northern cousins and will regularly spend each day in a different nest, although females will settle, after a forty-day gestation, in a permanent nest to give birth and rear up to nine youngsters.

Africa has representatives of all three genera of spiny hedgehogs. In the far north-eastern corner along the Mediterranean coast from Cyrenaica as far as Egypt and the Nile Valley lives the long-eared hedgehog *Hemiechinus auritus*. Like the desert hedgehog it lives in arid desert and scrubland and seldom drinks, probably obtaining most of its moisture from its prey of small vertebrates and insects. One pair, in fact, survived for ten weeks in a laboratory without food and water; but knowing from our wild casualties how difficult it is to counter the regressive effects of starvation and emaciation, I wonder if these two victims eventually succumbed to their own remarkable ability to go without. Smaller than the desert hedgehog, weighing only 500 grams, the long-eared hedgehog has cream-coloured spines with two slate-grey bands and with the same longitudinal grooves

Long-eared hedgehog, Hemiechinus auritus.

Brandt's hedgehog, Paraechinus hypomelas.

as its cousin. Its white face has some brown shading while its underside, legs and claws are completely white. It has longer ears than the desert hedgehog and these too are white.

The long-eared hedgehog breeds only once each year, between July and September, producing four to seven very small young in a burrow about 50 centimetres deep with a nest chamber in the deepest, coolest section.

With the desert hedgehogs, the long-eared hedgehogs must have been those of the Bible, for outside Africa their range covers all the Near and Middle East, as well as all of south-west Asia, south-eastern Europe and Cyprus right across southern Russian into Afghanistan, India and Mongolia.

To the east of Mongolia and the Gobi Desert into China and the realm of the moon rats is the domain of *Hemiechinus dauuricus*, the Daurian hedgehog. Very similar to the long-eared it manages to feed mainly on small rodents but very little is known about its way of life and breeding habits, except that it favours dry steppes.

It still surprises me that so little is known about some species of hedgehog, even those which have rubbed shoulders with man for many thousands of years. Another example is *Paraechinus hypomelas*, Brandt's hedgehog of Arabia. Found on islands in the Persian Gulf and on some mountains bordering the Arabian Sea, Brandt's hedgehog is almost completely black with some white hairs on its face. It has pale legs, and ears which are as large but slightly narrower than those of the desert hedgehog. Nothing is known of its habits and lifestyle.

The third member of the *Paraechinus* genera is the Indian hedgehog, *Paraechinus micropus*. Very similar in its lifestyle to the long-eared hedgehog it inhabits the hot, arid regions of the sub-continent. Very much a sedentary animal, it digs its own burrow in a sheltered place and uses that as a base for up to a year. Unlike other hedgehogs it will sometimes take food back to its nest for future use and, although it spends a passive period during the winter in some of the colder deserts, I doubt if it keeps food for this purpose. It breeds only once a year and produces only one or two young which indicates a higher success rate than other species in rearing offspring.

The last species of spiny hedgehog, of which once again not much is known, is *Erinaceus amurensis*, the Eastern Asiatic or Manchurian hedgehog. Living on forested grassland it is found in China and Korea and is possibly the only species of hedgehog that has been introduced to Japan.

The other five genera of hedgehogs are the *Echinosoricinae* or hairy hedgehogs of south-east Asia. The largest of the group, and incidentally the largest of the living insectivores, is *Echinosorex gymnurus*, the greater moon rat. Weighing in at up to 1400 grams it is the size of a rabbit. Its alternative name of *Gymnure*, meaning 'naked tail', aptly describes it but the 20 centimetre tail is covered with scales and compressed for one third of its length. The hedgehog's overall colour is black with whiter markings on its face, neck, shoulders and tail. Near to its anus it has two very powerful scent glands that emit an odour described as rotten onions, garlic or mouldy Irish stew, which can be detected from some distance away.

Strictly nocturnal and lying up under trees or bushes during the day, it tends to live near to water and does not hesitate to jump in to catch crustaceans, molluscs and, very often, fish. It is considered the most primitive of the insectivores and was found in Europe before the spiny hedgehogs took over. Now it is confined to the forests and mangrove swamps of Borneo, Sumatra, Malaysia, Thailand and Burma, where the tropical climate allows it to breed all the year round, producing two or three youngsters at a time.

The lesser moon rat, *Hylomys suillus*, also lives in the forests of south-east Asia, but has extended its range into Yunnan in China and into Java in the south. At only 10 to 12 centimetres long it is much smaller than its cousin, the greater moon rat, and searches for its prey, insects and earthworms, in short leaps and bounds on regularly used pathways. Not as handsome as its larger cousin it has a very short tail and is a rusty brown colour over all. It does, however, have the same malodorous anal glands.

Greater moon rat, Echinosorex gymnurus.

Lesser moon rat, Hylomys suillus.

A very close relative is *Neohylomys hainanensis*, the Hainan moon rat, from the Chinese island of Hainan. Not discovered until 1959, it is already threatened with extinction since the clearance of its forest home. Only a few specimens have been found which were slightly larger than the lesser moon rat. Its colouring is rusty brown and grey, with a black stripe down its back, dull yellow markings on its sides and a pale-coloured underside. Its feet, tail and ears have only a sprinkling of short hairs.

Another moon rat close to extinction because of 'slash and burn' forest clearance is the Mindanao moon rat, *Podogymnura truei*, of the Philippines. This 15-centimetre-long animal has been living in the mountain forests for centuries where the aboriginal natives, who know it as a 'bagobo' (meaning ground pig), trap it occasionally for food. It is interesting that the native word should have a meaning so similar to our own 'hedgehog' – the animals have remarkably similar eating habits. The moon rat has long, soft fur on its body and, although its tail is shorter than that of the greater moon rat, this too has a covering of brown hair.

The name shrew hedgehog aptly describes moon rats, but in particular is applied to *Neotetracus sinensis*,

Shrew hedgehog, Neotetracus sinensis.

the smallest of the *Echinosoricinae*, which lives in cool damp forests over 2000 metres up in northern Burma, Vietnam, Thailand and the Szechwan and Yunnan Provinces in China. Barely 20 centimetres long, including a long tail, it looks very similar to the lesser moon rat but in fact has fewer teeth and much finer fur. It probably feeds on the usual hedgehog fare of earthworms and grubs but may take some vegetable matter.

Its breeding habits are still the subject of some debate; it may be that the shrew hedgehog produces its four to five young during a long breeding season – April to September – or else has two shorter breeding periods – April and May or August and September. What is known is that for nesting it excavates burrows under stones, which it then lines with moss, and that any young have their eyes open in three weeks and can manage solid food after six weeks but carry on suckling until they are eight weeks old.

As far as the rain forest of south-east Asia, across the deserts of the Middle East and Africa and to the cold dark gardens of Europe: that's how far hedgehogs have managed to penetrate and survive. The visitor to your garden may not be an exotic moon rat but under that coat of prickles your neighbourhood hedgehog has the same pedigree.

Mindanao moon rat, Podogymnura truei.

Born Free

THE IDEA of going out to find your very own hedgehog is tempting – after all, it's an endearing creature and good for the garden – but the plan is much less attractive when you look at it from the animal's point of view.

Imagine ambling along, on a familiar ground, keeping a wary nose out for marauding badgers or dogs, trying hard to find enough food to build yourself up for the not too distant winter, looking forward to going home to your nest where five babies are waiting for your return, when, all of a sudden, thumping footsteps come through the grass towards you. You bring your spines over to protect your face but two giant gloved hands grip like a vice around your body. You roll into a ball but the hands grip tighter and you are falling into a cardboard box from which there is no way out. You feel yourself being carried and then dropped into a dark cavity. There is a strong smell of petrol; a lid closes with a click above you; a roar, a vibration and then a sense of moving very fast. Bouncing about in your cardboard box, you wonder how long you have been there; then as you stretch up, on your hind legs, to the top of the box, the moving stops and you are thrown forward. The lid opens, a bright light dazzles

you through the gap in your ball of spines. A lot of people gabble excitedly, then there's a hiss and a fine mist of something smelling abominably settles on your back and seeps into your eyes. You feel yourself being tipped out of the box and there's grass beneath your body. But where are you, where are your babies? You don't know any of these scents. There's a dog! But he only sniffs, thank goodness. Which way back home? Let's make a run for it – there's a wall in the way. Turn around, another wall; there's a wall in every direction, no way out. You cry silently and curl up in some leaves, full of despair, misery and hopelessness. This must be captivity.

Those feelings may be anthropomorphic – who knows? They may be fact and yet nobody does anything to prevent the heartless capture, and often despatch, of many hundreds of harmless hedgehogs every year.

It happens, not just occasionally with the taking of one hedgehog, but often *en masse*, masquerading as a scientific evacuation to protect one of man's whims. As recently as August 1986, as I was reading my daily paper before going outside to tend to the early feed of the orphaned hedgehogs tucked up

THE SUNDAY EXPRESS June 15 1986

Hedgehog heaven

Island where 2 pets became 10,000.

by JOHN CHAPMAN

POSTMAN John Tulloch was fed up with slugs ravaging his greenhouse plants.

So he decided to obtain two hedgehogs to eat the slugs and double up as pets for his children.

The trouble was there were no hedgehogs on the remote island of North Ronaldsay, in the Orkneys where Mr Tulloch lived.

So he brought back a couple —a male and a female—from the mainland.

That was in 1972.

Fourteen years later, Mr Tulloch's solution to his gardening troubles has led to a serious ecological problem on North Ronaldsay which is being urgently studied by scientists.

For shortly after they arrived on the island, Mr Tulloch's hedgehogs burrowed their way out of the greenhouse, went off and lived in the wilds.

Nature took is course . . . and now naturalists estimate there are 10,000 hedgehogs causing havoc to the island wildlife.

North Ronaldsay has a reputation as a bird sanctuary. But ornithologists have noticed a "drastic" reduction in the bird population which includes black headed gulls, terns, lapwings, oyster catchers, and wild ducks.

Dr Kevin Woodbridge, the island's GP and a keen ornithologist, told me : "The hedgehogs are decimating the bird population by eating birds' eggs.

"There are no predators here to control the hedgehog population. They have gone totally out of control."

Dr Jim Fowler, of the School of Life Sciences at Leicester Polytechnic, is leading an inquiry on the island, backed by funds from the British Hedgehog Preservation Society.

"The balance of nature has been upset on the island," he said. "We will see if the hedgehogs can be re-located."

A spokesman for the Hedgehog Preservation Society said : " We will give all the help we can.

" The hedgehogs might have to be transported off the island and taken back to the mainland.

" We certainly won't allow them to be killed."

Mr Tulloch, the 53-year-old postman who introduced the hedgehogs to North Ronaldsay, said : " It's all rather embarrassing. It's hard to believe I'm the person responsible for them being here."

Island's farewell to prickly problem

THE great hedgehog arlift gets under way today.

Dozens were due to be rounded up last night on the Orkney island of North Ronaldsay where they outnumber the 75 residents by ten to one.

Hedgehogs were first taken to the island 15 years ago to help control greenhouse pests. But they bred rapidly and some have been eating the eggs of rare birds.

The island's GP, Dr Kevin Woodbridge, said the captured hedgehogs would be flown to the mainland today rather than killed.

These newspaper articles brought St Tiggywinkles to the rescue of the Orkney hedgehogs.

Prickly problem for the Orkneys

By Ann Hills

NORTH Ronaldsay, the farthest-flung Orkney island, is suffering from a population explosion — among the hedgehogs.

About 1,000 of them, all descended from a single pair introduced by mistake in 1972, are menacing the local birds.

"They have decimated the population of young birds — 1,000 pairs of Arctic terns have only reared six fledglings this year," says Dr Kevin Woodbridge, the island's GP and an ornithologist.

The answer is to ship them out to good homes — if possible before the second litters are born in September, to avoid orphans.

But how. . .

warmly in St Tiggywinkles' intensive care unit, the headline hit me: 'Prickly Problem for the Orkneys'. I nearly choked at the stupidity, or was it callousness, of a prominent birdwatcher on the island of North Ronaldsay in the Orkneys off the north-west coast of Scotland who had decided, without the benefit of a prolonged independent study, that the island's population of hedgehogs had caused a catastrophic decline in the number of arctic duck eggs. Apparently the pair of hedgehogs which had been introduced to the island fourteen years before had proliferated to the extraordinary number of ten thousand by 1986. When faced with the sheer impossibility of this breeding capability, the numbers quoted were reduced to 1000, then 750, then 600. Nobody really knew the exact figure.

The charge was that the hedgehogs had been breaking into the terns' and ducks' eggs and lapping up the contents. It is a physical impossibility for a hedgehog to break into a duck's egg and unlikely that it could do damage to an unbroken tern's egg; its jaws are just too small and weak to be able to crack the shell. Other residents of the island – gulls, skuas, otters, rats and humans – are far more adept at removing or damaging eggs. The fallacy, as we have seen, is not a new one.

Without considering the facts, the birdwatcher openly condemned the hedgehogs. The slaughter of the Ronaldsay hedgehogs was advocated, since there was no law to stop it. Fortunately, however, fear of public opinion prevented the massacre. It was decided instead to round up all the hedgehogs and fly them to the mainland, regardless of the consequences.

The night before I read of their shenanigans, the round-up had started in spite of warnings that there were likely to be nests of hedgehog young which would die of starvation or hypothermia if their mothers were taken away. Forty-two had already been rounded up and dumped on the mainland. The perpetrators of this crime gave the excuse that they had segregated any pregnant or nursing mothers. Since it is impossible to tell whether a hedgehog is pregnant or lactating, we would say that at a very conservative estimate 25 per cent of those deposed hedgehogs were nursing mothers, which means that there could have been as many as 50 prematurely orphaned babies left behind to face the cold northern nights alone.

A phone call to the Nature Conservancy Council, the government watchdog on wildlife matters, achieved nothing. They were, they said, powerless. They had been threatened with the slaughter of the hedgehogs if they did not approve the evacuation. The hedgehogs were completely without protection but thankfully the threat of exposure by the media brought a lull in operations. But for how long?

The first whining hedgehog baby was soon picked up on the island and someone with a conscience made the first phone call to us: 'How do we rear this baby?' There were probably another 49 somewhere, suffering; but there were no terns – they had left the island months ago, having completed their breeding season. If the hedgehogs had to be moved, why couldn't the operation have waited until October or November, when there would have been no dependent youngsters?

The unfortunate 42 were apparently dumped on the mainland, in woods and on farmland without any consideration for their welfare or the effect on resident wildlife. The only modicum of legal protection available to the hedgehogs during this whole affair was that it would be classed as an offence or cruelty under the Abandonment of Animals Act

1960 to release an animal when it was likely to suffer unnecessarily because of that release. This would apply in the case of an unweaned hedgehog youngster being turned out to starve: I can only hope that this did not happen. In Britain, as we saw in Chapter 2, cruelty to a wild animal is not generally classed as an offence. However, once a wild animal or bird has been picked up, it automatically becomes the responsibility of whoever has it in captivity and it is subject to the Protection of Animals Act 1911, which does not protect *non-captive* wildlife – hence the tolerance by the law of the horrendous cruelty inflicted on foxes, stags and hares by the hunting fraternity.

The one glimmer of hope lies in the fact that the Ronaldsay hedgehogs were released at all: there is unfortunately a growing trend towards keeping hedgehogs as pets. Guinea pigs have been bred from captive animals for three thousand years and are conditioned to live in confinement. But go along to any old fashioned zoo and watch the tiger prowling up and down within the limits of its cage. Hopeless, lost, depressed and, perhaps most of all, bored, he cannot come to terms with the loss of freedom. A hedgehog is no different; he too is a wild animal – perhaps without the stature and charisma of a tiger – but he still needs to roam his mini-jungle endlessly searching for any tit-bits. Put him in a cage and he will prowl up and down, possibly injuring himself in his efforts to escape, and invariably he will die prematurely, seeming to give up the will to live. I have to keep injured hedgehogs, badgers, moles and foxes in cages or pens until they are fit to be released. If you were to go to any pen in the still of the night you would see them all striving, fighting, in spite of their injuries, to find a way of escape.

Surely it's more humane and I believe more re-warding to make friends with local hedgehogs, earn their trust and get to know a completely wild animal which doesn't flee at your approach. Gardens are their future, why not show them that yours is a haven, safe from insecticides and brimming over with all manner of creepy crawlies, with the added bonus of a nightly dish of dog or cat food as *hors d'oeuvre*.

'What! No bread and milk?' you ask. That's right, *no bread or milk*. No adult carnivore or insectivore would eat cereal or drink milk in the wild state. Their digestive systems have evolved to cope only with meat; they cannot successfully deal with anything else. A recent study of the contents of wild hedgehog droppings showed some vegetable matter, but most of it was passed in an undigested state: the hedgehogs had wasted their time eating it. So bread is no good for them, but milk is even worse: it contains lactose, which neither hedgehogs nor for that matter cats can digest and which remains an ideal growing medium for bacteria of all kinds. Give a hedgehog regular feeds of cow's milk and it will soon develop diarrhoea which could result in dehydration, emaciation and often death.

Yet somehow the hedgehog seems to know which food is beneficial to him and, as Wroot in his paper published by the Mammal Society has proved, shows a preference for its natural prey, for those grubs and insects with the higher nutritional value. Watch a hedgehog on its nightly rounds: notice how it ignores a bread and milk offering for most of the night, tending to treat it as a dessert which it will come to but of which it will only drink a small amount. A survey, with miniature radio monitors, on the nightly roaming of a group of hedgehogs showed that none of them, on leaving their daytime nests, went directly to the bread and milk regularly

The hedgehog makes a very unhappy pet.

put out for them. They had so little regard for the additional food source that none of them even bothered to nest near to that garden. In fact, whether bread or milk was there made no difference to their pattern of behaviour. Yet, if that bread and milk had been replaced with good wholesome meat, I am sure that many of the hedgehogs would have made a beeline for the feast and would have been so full after gorging themselves that they would have rested close by and might even have built themselves a temporary nest and in due course might have become permanent residents of the garden.

The first way to a hedgehog's heart is through its stomach and nothing is more enticing to a hedgehog than the scent of a good meal that is both attractive and of high nutritional value. We find that tinned dog or cat food is both convenient and appreciated by the hedgehogs. The mushier the better is the rule, with Co-op Supermeat and Pedigree Chum Puppy Food receiving top marks in the hedgehogs' Egon Ronay Guide. They are particularly fond of liver, especially liver-flavoured dog food, with raw mince, meat offal and chicken running a close second. If your neighbourhood hedgehog will not come to eat, offer a tin of pilchards: the smell may well be irresistible. Now and again the occasional digestive biscuit adds variety and one of our permanent residents, the blind Earthquake, likes raw peanuts in the shell taken from the buried larder of Chestnut, St Tiggywinkles' resident squirrel. I should imagine in Nairobi, where the gardens have visits by four-toed hedgehogs and where there may be peanuts growing in the vegetable patch, these would make a tasty follow-up to a night's feasting on East African caterpillars and beetles.

Any kind of meat, even the left-over bone from the dinner table, is welcomed but it is dangerous to offer any animal pork either cooked or uncooked. One of the most acceptable morsels, although the idea may seem ghoulish, is the dead mouse which the cat has brought in. But make sure that it has not been the victim of poisoning.

The Germans, true hedgehog fans, can even buy hedgehog food, *Igelfutter*, in their local supermarkets. Perhaps one of our petfood manufacturers should look into this new market potential; it would, at last, do away with that old fallacy about bread and milk.

Hedgehogs live up to their name: with their lip-smacking, walking-in-their-food way of eating they can wolf down up to 20 per cent of their own body weight in a single night. Coupled with this they like to drink copious amounts of water – as much as a third of a litre at a time – so make sure that there is always fresh water available. In the very hot dry summer of 1984 many hundreds of hedgehogs were saved from fatal dehydration by bowls of water put out when all the natural water supplies had dried up.

Unlike wild birds which come to rely on supplementary feeding in the garden, hedgehogs do not interrupt their natural feeding rhythms to visit feeding stations and will not suffer, only sometimes show annoyance, if you should forget or be unable to put out food. However, I think that regular feeding during the winter should not be interrupted until the hedgehogs go into hibernation and cease to appear.

Hedgehogs do not have very good eyesight and prefer to keep to the security of the garden boundaries and, once again unlike birds, hedgehogs will appreciate their food being placed close to a boundary fence or wall, even the house wall where you will be able to watch their comings and goings from the comfort of a window. They may even get used

A mother hedgehog may even bring her family to a tempting bowl of dog food.

to the house lights but will shy away from sudden noise or movement like the drawing of curtains or slamming of a door.

If you should try to photograph your visiting hedgehog, especially with a single lens reflex camera, you will soon see that it instantly pulls forward its forehead spines at the sound of the shutter or mirror moving. Most photographs taken without the high speed exposure of electronic flash will show a hedgehog well on its way to curling up. The only sure way to photograph one so that you can at least see its eyes is by using synchronised flash, preferably with a 135 mm lens. The hedgehog will not be disturbed by the flash and it will freeze any movement before the hedgehog has a chance to frown.

There have been reports of hedgehogs becoming so trusting as to come when called or when their food dish is tapped. By calling each time you put out food or rattling the dish, you may well be able to rely on some hedgehogs turning up on demand. However, this technique would take a long time and a great deal of patience to achieve results but, as with any relationship built up with a wild animal, you feel honoured to be allowed to share its trust, if only at feeding time.

Of course, with all this food lying around at night you will no doubt attract some of the neighbourhood cats, who will see your feeding station as a welcome break from mouse-hunting. They pose no threat to an adult hedgehog, although a juvenile may be vulnerable. Often sharing the same feeding bowl as hedgehogs, they have, unfortunately, the typical cat habit of cleaning the plate, leaving none for late-comers. The hedgehog characteristic which lets you know that one has called is to turn the plate over, presumably to look for millipedes or worms underneath. An empty plate the right way up shows that cats have emptied it but one upside down points to hedgehogs having beaten them to it.

Nobody has perfected a simple system to keep cats at bay, but the Henry Doubleday Research Association have a design that works remarkably well. One of their members, Mrs P. Kenyon, uses a wire mesh basket turned upside down with one side overlapping the other, forming an angled entrance which for some reason cats find impossible to negotiate but which hedgehogs can get into, although with some difficulty. Another anti-cat feeding station which also works – on the principle that hedgehogs can and like to squeeze through the smallest of gaps – is another inverted wire basket with a small arch just two inches high and four inches wide cut in the rim – which is all that's needed to keep cats out but let hedgehogs in.

Hedgehogs love to poke those long mobile noses under anything that hints at food. Put a tin lid over a dish of meat and the cats will be flummoxed but the hedgehogs will simply nose it off. If ever you

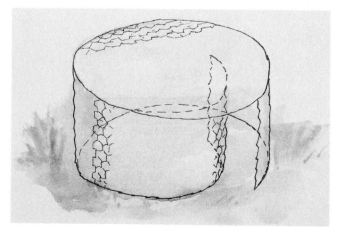

A hedgehog feeding station which deters cats.

have to put out the hedgehog fodder before nightfall, the lid will prevent any birds depriving the hedgehogs of their supper. Blackbirds and starlings in particular are very partial to tinned food: in fact, we raise all our baby bird orphans on Pedigree Chum Puppy Food.

Don't be discouraged if despite all this preparation hedgehogs do not appear as soon as it gets dark. They love to roam and may cover as much as two miles in a night and, with constant interruptions to snuffle piles of old leaves or munch on a millipede, it may take some hours for them to reach your feeding station. Even the females, who tend not to roam as far as the boars, will travel 500 metres every night. Quite unlike the foxes, robins and moles which may visit your garden, hedgehogs do not maintain clearly defined territories nor do they follow regular routes as they forage for food. Try to intercept a meandering hedgehog with your offer of good food. Although it is not a guaranteed attraction, the scent may well persuade the hedgehog that your garden is a good area in which to set up home.

Mere food is not enough for some hedgehogs. They have very specific requirements if they are to settle in an area. They like a prolific supply of thick hedges and shrubs under which they can hide and a regular supply of fallen leaves and grasses which they can carry away in their mouths – not on their spines as some writers would have us believe – to build and line their nests. A garden reeking of pesticides, devoid of any invertebrate life under the canopy of fallen leaves, would not be of much interest to a hedgehog. If there is enough to keep it interested, a foraging hedgehog will snuffle about for most of the night, only returning to its nest just before dawn and probably picking a site not too far away.

Why not offer them somewhere to nest? Nothing could be better than a nice thick berberis or bramble, bamboo or pampas grass, where they can feel secure. In particular they like to nest against a wall or fence, under an established ivy or other evergreen climber. During the summer the lush thick growth of cotoneaster or the base of the prolific deciduous climbers, honeysuckle and russian vine, would look extremely inviting to a tired, over-full hedgehog, with the added attraction that there would always be a constant supply of leaves for nest-building.

Our visiting hedgehogs like nothing better than to squeeze under the small timber building that was St Tiggywinkles' first surgery. Administering first aid to a casualty late in the evening I could always hear the residents, below floor, stirring and having their first good scratch before venturing out into the garden. Another great favourite of hedgehogs is the compost heap; and a pile of logs with a gap underneath may prove irresistible to a hedgehog. But why not build them something more substantial so that you know where they are and can avoid accidentally disturbing them?

Capital Radio in association with the London Wildlife Trust came up with the idea of sinking an upturned plastic milk crate, with its partitions cut out and a 11 centimetre entrance hole cut in one end, under a small rockery incorporating any old bricks, stones or bits of wood that so often litter untidy corners of the garden. Small alpine plants and wall-living species, like the linarias and sedums, should thrive in well drained soil, adding a splash of colour to that wasted corner, and, you never know, a hedgehog may well find the underneath just as attractive and move in.

As a follow up to their cat-preventative basket the Henry Doubleday Research Association designed a more salubrious hedgehog nest box that was also

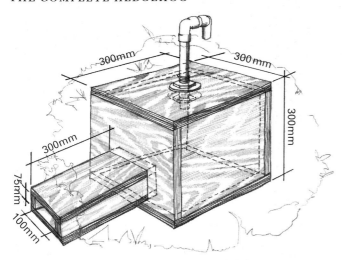

A secure nest box suitable for a nursery or for hibernation.

guaranteed to exclude cats but perhaps more importantly offered some protection, especially for hibernating hedgehogs, from the occasional passing and ever-hungry badger. It can be built from any cheap *untreated* timber and it has a tunnel entrance, to keep out unwanted visitors, and a ventilation pipe to ensure a free circulation of air. A resident hedgehog will invariably fill the box with leaves, grass and even old newspapers, so the inside end of the ventilation pipe should be kept clear with a cowl of small-gauge wire netting. Place the box in a quiet sheltered part of the garden and cover it with a polythene sheet before burying it under compost or soil which will add essential insulation during the colder nights of winter.

You may be lucky for, although hedgehogs are solitary animals, sometimes more than one will adopt the same winter quarters. At St Tiggywinkles we regularly find groups of rehabilitating patients cuddled up, not in the provided nest boxes, but underneath them where they dig dormitories for themselves.

Let's now assume that you have hedgehogs regularly coming into your garden, taking advantage of the ready meals and superb accommodation. They know your scent, they know your voice, they may even trust you, but you know nothing about them, not even whether they are male or female. You could pick one up but even if you managed to unroll it, would you know what to look for, and would you risk frightening it away for ever?

It's not too difficult to learn the intimate secrets of your hedgehog but it does take time and infinite amounts of patience. The first thing you should do is to get a pair of fairly thick gloves. Hedgehogs can be remarkably prickly to pick up and to drop one is fatal to the relationship you have built up. Put the gloves on, approach the hedgehog slowly; talk to it, let it know you are there and then let it sniff your hands. Do not attempt to pick it up at this stage for, if it rolls into a ball, there is almost no way you can force it to unroll and, once again, you will destroy its hard-won trust.

If it does not shy away from you, slowly slide your hands, palms uppermost, under its stomach and gently lift it. There will be fleas but even if they jump on to you they will not stay and will not bite so there is no need to worry about them. Your hedgehog may well relax and simply kick with its legs; if so, slide your hands right under it, being extremely careful not to drop it. Then put it down again with its nose in the food dish. Even if it does not unroll completely, put it down and try again the next day. After three or four evenings of this gentle coaxing you should be able to pick up your hedgehog without any fear of it closing up. There are, of course, hedgehogs which will never relax and some-

Patches – star of St Tiggywinkles.

times, when casualties arrive at St Tiggywinkles, we have to resort to quicker methods of unrolling them. In our situation we are fortunate in having the world's first anaesthetic machine designed purely for unrolling hedgehog casualties for preliminary examination of their injuries. You will not have this luxury so you will have to resort to more devious means of unrolling your unwilling hedgehog. Legend has it that the cunning old fox rolls his intended hedgehog victim into water, where it has to uncurl to save itself from drowning. Nobody has ever seen this happen and I do not think we should resort to such a method.

The method I use with fairly co-operative patients is to lift them from underneath and then gently to rock them backwards and forwards. The motion seems to make them somewhat giddy so that they gradually unroll to see what is going on. As they do

73

so I slowly slide more fingers under their soft belly until they are completely relaxed. However, make one sudden move, touch the nose or the wrong guard hair and you have to start again with an impregnable ball of prickles.

They will also relax if you stroke their spines from head to tail gradually pulling the spines back from the head. Some practitioners say you should grip one of the head spines with a pair of forceps and force the head back but I usually find gentle persuasion has a far more lasting effect without causing the hedgehog any discomfort.

When you have unrolled a hedgehog, you would have to look at its underside in order to establish its gender but if you simply turn it over you're back at the beginning again with a tightly curled ball. With your right hand flat under its chest and your left hand under its rump, place each thumb on top of the hedgehog, flattening the spines and feel how, as you turn it, you can resist its attempts to curl up. Now lean the hedgehog back against your stomach and peer down, over its chin, and note the position of the sexual organs: quite easily differentiated, the male's is right in the middle of its abdomen, while the female's is hard to see, being situated far to the back of the animal in front of the anal opening. Quickly check it for injuries then hurriedly put it down with its nose, once again, in the food dish.

'Marvellous,' I hear you say, 'but how can we identify our visiting hedgehog once we have decided on its sex?' I find it fairly easy to identify familiar hedgehogs – a broken patch of spines or a light patch, or even a peculiar way of approaching the food dish, and of course there's Pinky, a partial albino, with a bright pink nose. I am not in favour of marking hedgehogs with spray paint or nail varnish or any other substance. Paint could easily set up a skin irritation and to hedgehogs, with their superb sense of smell, these chemicals must be overpowering and could affect their interchange with other hedgehogs.

It's a challenge to coax hedgehogs into your own garden. Once there, they will stay. But if you pick up a hedgehog elsewhere to put it into your garden, it will eventually escape and find its way back to its original home.

John Lamming, in 1981, found that on Brownsea Island hedgehogs which were moved to various parts of the island always made their way home, often swimming expanses of water on the way. Sometimes they returned overnight and one took 29 days but, although they ran from the release sites at an average of 466 metres per hour, when they reached their home range they slowed to 180 metres per hour and started to forage. They obviously knew where they were going, just like the injured European hedgehog which took two months to travel the 48 miles from Dimitrovsk to its original home in the eastern Ukraine. However, don't think of bringing a hedgehog back into Britain from abroad as it is subject to the anti-rabies law and would have to suffer six months' quarantine.

Ben Brown

Everything in the Garden is . . .

THE SCENE is a sitting room, overlooking the garden of a bungalow in a small town in Buckinghamshire. I am sitting, waiting by the French windows having been called to see one of the garden's regular visitors which, it's thought, might need treatment at the Wildlife Hospital. With no warning, at the very limit of the patio lights, a small black and white striped face suddenly appears over the mound that is the lawn. A pause, then boldly the first badger lollops across to the window and with much lip-smacking and teeth-grinding tucks into the plate of food, so near that I feel I can almost reach out and touch her. Luckily a badger's eyesight is not very good so she is unaware of me sitting behind the glass just above her. Another badger bulldozes his way into the feast: this is obviously the dominant boar I had been waiting to see.

All of a sudden, silently, a fox appears over the rise. Keeping to the shadows as foxes do so well, he has obviously scented the food now being demolished by the badgers. Warily he paces up and down but the sow badger senses his presence and with a charge sends him scurrying elsewhere for his supper.

Other badgers materialise out of the darkness. Soon there are five of them, waiting their turn for the food, that is if the big boar leaves anything for them. It is a sight never to be forgotten.

Every garden can have its own wildlife showcase, perhaps not with VIP players like badgers and foxes but with some of the smaller animals giving regular nightly performances to supplement the antics of the daytime visitors to the bird table. Like the birds, the smaller mammals, especially the hedgehog, will help themselves to insects and grubs, making enormous inroads into the so-called 'pest' population of a garden.

The naturalised European hedgehog in New Zealand has been found to control the major grassland pests, porina moths and grass grubs, so effectively that it has been accepted as one of the world's few successful introductions to another country. The ability to control up to 40 per cent of the adult insect population is just one example of the hedgehog's potential in our gardens. With just a little protection, hedgehogs will repay your concern by dealing with vast numbers of the insects and grubs which cause nightmares to gardeners, while at the same time obviating the need for the chemical warfare which eventually kills everything, friend and foe alike.

The hedgehog's preferred diet reads like a 'Who's Who' of the gardener's hit-list. But just how reliable are the claims of their prowess in clearing a garden of pests?

Take slugs for instance: everybody believes that

hedgehogs live on slugs. It is obviously important to find out whether or not they do, and if they *don't*, to discover what else they eat and how effective they are as predators. First, if we look objectively at the habits of the slug we see, once again, that we have been duped, or most slugs are not the villains everyone would have us believe they are. True, they will damage newly planted spring seedlings but their diet for the rest of the year consists of dead and decaying vegetable, and sometimes animal matter. They will turn their attention to cabbages only if your garden is so clean and tidy that there is no other food available. Even then they will not kill your plants but will merely leave a few holes as evidence of their presence, surely an insufficient crime to warrant their wholesale slaughter. Come to think of it, hedgehogs would also go without a meal in a picture-book garden and would probably call only once.

Why not put some old rhubarb leaves in between the rows of vegetables and watch the slugs gather under them for protection? These slug shelters may not always be the first port of call for your neighbourhood hedgehogs but local slow-worms will relish any of the small grey slugs, *Limax agrestis*, they can find and an added bonus may be visits from the now rare glow-worms whose larvae feed avidly on small slugs and snails.

Those vulnerable newly planted seedlings can be protected by surrounding them with spiky suckers cut from rose bushes, nettles, brambles, in fact anything that will act as a painful barrier to the tender-footed slugs and snails.

Hedgehogs, like blackbirds, will occasionally resort to a meal of slugs, particularly in the autumn. *Arion hortensis*, the garden slug, seems to be a particular favourite but the large black slug, *Arion ater*, may

be a little too tough. *Milax gracilis*, the slim black sheep of the family, does a lot of damage to potato crops in the autumn and being underground can escape the attention of the ground predators, centipedes, ground beetles and devil's coach horses, but digging in 500 grams of copper sulphate mixed with 3.5 kilograms of lime at a rate of 125 grams per square metre is an old remedy that will help maintain the equilibrium.

Snails occasionally feature on the hedgehog menu but these are only the thin-shelled varieties less than 19 millimetres in diameter.

Unlike the British hedgehogs and their cousins on the grasslands, the town and suburb dwelling hedgehogs of New Zealand have come to rely on slugs and snails as a crucial food source, which is probably just as well since the Europeans responsible for introducing the hedgehogs also accidentally brought in the unwelcome gastropods in the first place. I would be interested to know if these New Zealand hedgehogs wipe off the slug's slime with their front feet as the European hedgehogs do.

Although I have found references to the hedgehog's predation of moth larvae on the New Zealand grasslands I have seen very little comment on the important role hedgehogs play in keeping down numbers of moth larvae in European gardens. You may not think the moth larva does much damage to plants, unless you already know that this is another name for the cut-worm, a major garden nuisance which attacks plants, especially vegetables, at or around ground level. The larvae of these moths – the turnip moth, the heart and dart moth, the yellow underwing and their relatives – form nearly a quarter of the British hedgehog's diet, especially in April when the cut-worms are most active on the newly planted seed beds. Eating its fill twice nightly a

Hedgehogs and cats will often share the same food bowl.

hedgehog can dispose of thirty cut-worms each day as well as any caterpillars within reach, including those of the infamous cabbage white butterfly.

Since insectivores rely on catching numerous single items of prey, you would think that hedgehogs would plump for the slow, bulky slugs, snails and cut-worms which are suited to their own slow, deliberate hunting techniques, but in fact they seem to exist on a balanced diet. When there is a choice they will pick on those creatures with the highest nutritional value, even if it means catching fleet-footed beetles. When it meets a slow-moving creature or even a potential meal of carrion, the hedgehog will inspect it and sniff at it before laboriously munching its way through it; but if a tasty beetle goes whizzing by, the hedgehog will grab at it in an instant, clasping its teeth around the abdomen and crunching it up, often leaving only the hard elytra and jaws.

These beetles feature as part of the hedgehog's diet throughout most of the year but, possibly because the hedgehog fears a nip from the powerful jaws, it appears to ignore the predatory Carabid beetle which itself preys on many slugs and cut-worms. The vegetarian beetles are the hedgehog's speciality, particularly the strawberry seed beetle, seventy-five of which were found to have been eaten by one hedgehog at a sitting.

Weevils are another type of beetle regularly eaten by hedgehogs, as are the chafer beetles and their larvae, especially the bulky cockchafer, whose larvae can cause a great deal of damage to vegetable roots. A study carried out in May in the Ukraine discovered that the cockchafer forms the mainstay of the spring diet of both the Eastern and long-eared hedgehogs. The long-eared, *Hemiechinus auritus*, also uses its digging prowess to uncover fat juicy chafer grubs.

Not many people realise that the well-known wire-worm is the larval form of another beetle, the click beetle, which jumps in the air with a loud click if it is laid on its back. (There goes another fallacy – that beetles die if they are turned over.) The click beetle is another hedgehog favourite, the larva as well as the adult beetle. These can be found in the staggering proportions of over two million per acre. They love potatoes and will destroy most of the crop if nothing is done to stem the onslaught. Even the hedgehog and its allies would be hard-pressed to have any effect on these millions, but there are ways of helping the hedgehog and saving your potatoes without resorting to expensive and dangerous chemicals. Wire-worms prefer to feed on the dead and decaying roots of grasses and weeds and will flock to buried perforated tins filled with old potato peelings or pieces of potato. Digging up the tins at regular intervals will provide a supply of captured wire-worms, which are ideal as a supplement for the bird table.

Not all beetle larvae are nuisances. The ladybird larva, which looks like a miniature crocodile, is a great friend of the gardener and in its adult form is both a good predator and a firm favourite with everybody except hedgehogs. Their natural insect chemical repellent seems to be particularly effective and ladybirds are one of the few beetles ignored by hedgehogs. The arrangement is a convenient one for, while the hedgehog hunts at ground level, the ladybird and its offspring wreak havoc amongst the aphids sucking at the growing tips of many plant species.

It is not simply the acrid taste of the ladybird's chemical repellent which deters the hedgehog, for hedgehogs are reputed to overlook completely the potent poison emitted by the oil and blister beetles.

Hedgehogs love to forage amongst leaf litter and toadstools.

Hedgehogs are not put off by a toad's 'blow-up' display or its unpleasant taste.

Since this can repel even humans and other larger mammals, it is not unreasonable to fear that hedgehogs will happily eat grubs and other creatures which have been doused with toxic insecticides.

One beetle which does not need a chemical defence to protect it, even against a hedgehog, is the fearsome devil's coach horse, the large black beetle which raises its tail just like a scorpion. But unlike a scorpion the coach horse's weapon is not on its tail but at its front end – powerful jaws which make even me wary of picking it up and which keep the hedgehog, with its soft vulnerable nose, at a safe distance. The coach horse is a great ally of the gardener, preying on anything small enough to be captured by those lethal jaws.

Sometimes, however, natural chemical deterrents fail to put off a predator and may even prove to be a handicap. The chemical secretions of the millipede which damages plants at ground level seem to attract the hedgehog even from some distance away. It may repel smaller predators but the millipede, with an extra layer of fat under its chitinous skin, features prominently on the hedgehog's 'good food guide'. The fast-moving centipede – different from the millipede in having one pair of legs per body segment as opposed to two pairs per segment – is itself an efficient predator and in most cases can use its speed to evade capture by the hedgehog.

Most people know that the centipede is the gardener's ally, but some insects – usually if there is a commercial product on sale to control them – are branded pests even before the benefit of their presence has been considered. Just mention the word 'earwig' and people shudder in horror and reach for the insecticide, but in fact earwigs spend most of their time crawling into nooks and crevices to devour the insects which are too small for hedgehogs to catch. Scale insects, diptera flies and aphids feature in the earwig's diet, so their occasional chewing of dahlia and chrysanthemum leaves is surely excusable in view of the beneficial work they do in your garden.

Unfortunately for earwigs, they are a firm favourite of hedgehogs especially in New Zealand where P. A. Campbell found that they formed an important part of the hedgehog's diet. Not quite so crucial to the hedgehog in Britain, earwigs are nonetheless a regular part of their diet. Imagine the effect on the hedgehog if these earwigs have suffered a dose of insecticide because we believe them to be pests.

Together with earwigs, caterpillars, beetles and millipedes make up the bulk of a hedgehog's diet, with slugs featuring only later in the year, especially from October onwards when the hedgehog's other prey are no longer active.

You might imagine that earthworms, reputedly rich in protein, would be a fairly easily obtainable source of nourishment for hedgehogs, but they seem to prefer other foods. However, when they happen upon a worm they have been seen to sway from side to side before gripping the worm, always from the rear, and gradually chewing their way along it. Occasionally they will stop and bite the worm along its length before returning to the rear to start feeding again.

The natural balance seems to be in operation here, with hedgehogs taking only occasional earthworms which are the staple diet of moles and badgers. Similarly, hedgehogs do not eat many woodlice, which remain the domain of that other four-legged garden pest-controller, the shrew. Mind you, if food is scarce the hedgehog will not hesitate to catch woodlice and will even eat the shrew itself, if it can be caught. Once again the hedgehog shows its lack of dietary discrimination, as hardly any other animal will eat a shrew; in fact the neighbourhood cats kill and leave many lying around – a bonus for any foraging hedgehog.

All through the gardening months the hedgehog adds to its list of conquests: in midsummer it eats crane flies and their larvae, the leatherjackets; ants, which do no harm other than to disturb the roots of plants, are taken just before their nuptial flights; and froghoppers, which produce the frothy cuckoo spit so often seen lurking on plant stems, have no hiding place. The hedgehog digs for the minute nematodes, eelworms, which congregate around the roots of plants, giving many people the impression that it is trying to feed on the roots. Even that pioneer of natural history observation, the Reverend Gilbert White, writing to Thomas Pennant two hundred years ago, described how hedgehogs ate the roots of plantain on his grassed walks. He commented that 'with their upper mandible, which is longer than the lower, they bore under the plant, and so eat the roots off upwards'. He obviously did not appreciate that the sub-soil pests for which the hedgehogs were digging had probably already eaten any roots. Lord Tennyson in 'Aylmer's Field', published in 1864, mentioned the practice:

'The Hedgehog underneath the plantain bores'

but, wisely, he did not pass comment on its purpose.

Hedgehogs take in some vegetable matter but, in the main, this is swallowed incidentally, contained in the stomachs of its prey. Usually it passes through without further digestion.

None of us would miss the flies and maggots which hedgehogs dispose of, but unfortunately they also eat the occasional bee, as Doris Wright vividly confirmed in the *Countryman Wildlife Book*. After rescuing a hedgehog from a cattle grid she released it, whereupon it promptly ran into a swarm of bees, ate some, backed off and then ran in for more. She could not make out whether or not the spikes on its snout were bee stings.

As we have recently seen in the Orkneys, there is a perpetual debate about whether or not hedgehogs are seriously harmful to the eggs of ground-nesting birds, but this should not concern the gardener as hedgehogs are quite unable to climb to the nests of our familiar blackbirds, thrushes and finches. It will, however, dig out the contents of a mouse or rat nest, perhaps another bonus for the gardener who has been losing seed to the rodents. Any unwary toad will be taken but frogs are too fast to be caught and a slow-worm, grabbed by the tail, will simply shed it leaving the hedgehog with the frantically wriggling stub while the slow-worm slides off to safety under a rock.

Much has been written about the hedgehog and its battle with adders. Apparently it tries to kill and eat adders, although it will not approach the harmless grass snake. There are many reports of hedgehogs' supposed immunity to viper venom: M. Lenz was callous enough to introduce adders into a box with a nursing mother, reporting how the hedgehog attacked the snakes, seizing them by their heads. He then reported how a wild hedgehog seized an adder, was bitten several times but then, when the snake was exhausted, ate it, suffering no ill effects from the encounter. Frank Buckland in his notes to the Reverend Gilbert White's *Natural History of Selborne* described how a viper struck a hedgehog two or three times in the face while the hedgehog was biting the viper's tail. Again the hedgehog is supposed to have suffered no after-effects.

These reports, if true, sound like naïve hedgehog tactics; the popular version of the way in which a hedgehog attacks an adder is that he approaches the snake with a quick bite and, in an instant, retracts his face behind his forehead spines. The adder then strikes the spines which are longer than its fangs. Repeated retaliatory strikes by the adder on to that impenetrable barrier of sharp spines leave it mortally wounded, allowing the hedgehog to move in and finish its attack. It is possible that hedgehogs adopt these tactics in order to prey on adders but, as with so many hedgehog stories, there can be room for doubt.

In the past, German scientists have claimed that hedgehogs are immune to most poisons, but one report by a German, which tells how a captive animal survived being given prussic acid, arsenic, opium and a corrosive sublimate, shows how unreliable some scientific papers can be. Unfortunately the fallacy that hedgehogs enjoy a certain toxin immunity has been carried down through generations, with the tragic result that many animals die from gardeners' chemicals which are supposed to do them no harm.

Many people have questioned whether slug pellets may not be harmful to their local hedgehogs and have invariably been fobbed off with the story that the doses are so small that only the slugs suffer. As we have seen, hedgehogs eat other creatures in preference to slugs but the fact that all of these creatures may have insecticide in them has been virtually ignored by even the most caring gardener. It was proved, in the 1950s, that organo-chlorine compounds could build up in a predator eventually causing breeding defects and becoming a threat to its very existence. Yet today many of these chemicals are still on sale and are sprayed willy-nilly on crops, flowers, paths and vegetables with little or no thought for the fact that they can build up to lethal intensities which kill both garden friends and pests and on occasion even the gardener himself.

Many agricultural crops are routinely doused with chemicals whether there is evidence of insect damage or not. Called calendar spraying, it involves the same treatment year in, year out. The tragedy is that often there is no need to resort to expensive insecticides, but once you have started it is very difficult to stop. The garden is a living body and if left unmolested the natural balance between prey (the pests) and predator will keep infestation well under control, although there may be the occasional cabbage leaf with a hole chewed in it or a flower with a few petals missing. But isn't it refreshing to know that you can eat the cabbage without taking in chemical residues and can smell the flower without being overcome by the build up of toxic fumes, and that the garden is safe for hedgehogs, butterflies, birds, bees and other creatures?

However, if you use a chemical spray just once the balance is disturbed. You may have killed two thousand greenfly but you will also have killed the ladybirds, lacewings and hoverflies which prey on them. The greenfly shrug off the setback and breed with renewed vigour, but the predators do not have their breeding propensity and take much longer to recover. The greenfly multiply unhindered and before long there are more than ever. Another spraying merely kills some of them together with the surviving predators. So it goes on until you have the largest crop of greenfly imaginable, which even your sprays cannot destroy. Added to this, all the spray which missed the greenfly has fallen onto the flowers, vegetables and the soil, poisoning many other small creatures, killing some but touching others which can crawl off to become lethal prey for hedgehogs and any surviving predatory insects.

This carries on day after day, not just in your garden but also in that of your neighbours and their neighbours until eventually the amount of toxin taken in by your natural allies has reached a fatal limit. They die and are quickly eaten by the scavengers which, in turn, are eaten by the next generation of predators which die as a result. Meanwhile the greenfly just keep reproducing until your garden has no other wildlife.

To make matters worse, future greenfly generations may well acquire a resistance to some chemicals, just as many rats have become resistant to warfarin poison. When giant mutant rats started to appear in sewers, the instant easy solution was to use a more potent poison, difenacoum. Immediately the already threatened barn owl population started to nose dive; hedgehogs, cats and dogs scavenging on rat or mouse carcasses began to fall by the wayside. Warfarin did not necessarily kill the larger predators and there was always the chance of immediate vitamin injections to save a hedgehog, but there seems to be no defence against this new difenacoum and already conservation bodies are gloomy about the prognosis for other wild animals and birds.

Even the trapping of rats and mice can cause its problems: I deal with many hundreds of hedgehogs with broken or amputated legs or snouts – all the result of encounters with break-back traps intended for rodents. Planting some of the more aromatic mints – peppermint, penny royal and catmint – will keep rodents as well as ants and cabbage white butterflies at bay. But keep the plants in pots or they will eventually overrun your garden.

The stupidity of the supposed 'custodians of the countryside' never ceases to amaze me. Through their gamekeepers and farm workers they have all but wiped out most of the natural enemies of rats, mice and of course rabbits. Pine martens, polecats, buzzards, kites and barn owls just hang on to existence while the real champion rodent controllers – foxes, stoats and weasels – are labelled vermin to be destroyed however inhumanely. Together with the hedgehogs, which have nothing to fear from their carnivorous allies, these animals could once again restore the natural balance.

It is true that rats, mice and rabbits can cause a lot of damage to stored or growing crops, but so many of the other so-called pests do only cosmetic damage except where an occasional species may find conditions so ideal that it runs riot. But in this case, instead of using the broad-spectrum methods of control, why not be specific in your attack, without damaging innocent bystanders? Be very, very careful, however. The chemical generally recommended for use against wire-worm infestation of potatoes is gamma-BHC, but how many people I wonder ever read the small print which says it must not be used on edible crops? There are alternatives – diazinon, pirimphos-methyl or bromophos – all of which are labelled 'dangerous to all animals and birds', while the first two are suspected of causing birth or genetic defects to the user though this is never stated on the label. Just imagine what hedgehogs would be born if their parents had picked up any quantity of wireworms or any other creature poisoned, but not necessarily killed, by these chemicals. Of course you can use gamma-BHC on your flower beds, not on your edible crops. It will without exception kill the weevils, beetles, aphids, thrips, red spider mite, ladybirds, hedgehogs, robins – need I go on? Oh yes, it is also suspected of causing cancer in the user together with birth and genetic defects and has, in fact, been banned in more environmentally conscious countries like Sweden. Before we condemn it we ought to look at the crimes its victims commit: the red spider mite turns cherry tree leaves yellow; some beetle larvae may damage roots while others have the audacity to catch slugs and leatherjackets; aphids suck the sap of plants causing some slowing down of growth but the ladybirds, hoverflies and lacewings, condemned along with them, could, as we have seen, keep them under control; and finally thrips damage some pea flowers and pods. Are these really capital offences warranting lethal poisoning by gamma-BHC?

Although the damage done by moth caterpillars, cut-worms (the hedgehog's favourite food), is minimal and mainly cosmetic, it is often recommended that they be subjected to poisoning with diazinon, gamma-BHC, pirimphos-methyl and a new villain, carbaryl, which has the same hideous traits as gamma-BHC. Cut-worms may be a nuisance to the seedlings and young plants in a nursery bed but wrapping each plant with a bio-degradable cardboard collar will protect them until they are large enough to resist the insects' attentions.

Seeds and seedlings always seem to be at risk so it's a good idea when sowing to sprinkle them with garlic to keep away the millipedes, and any vampires which may be around! With this preventative and the help of the local hedgehogs there should be no need to resort to diazinon.

Leatherjackets cause bare patches on lawns – for which heinous crime it is recommended they be killed off with gamma-BHC, putting at risk the hedgehogs, shrews and starlings which gratuitously spike our lawns to hunt the tough little grubs. Watering and covering the bare patches with black poly-

thene will bring many leatherjackets to the surface, producing a veritable feast for the garden birds when the polythene is removed after a few hours. Turning over cultivated soil in the winter will also bring many leatherjackets and other grubs to the attention of the neighbourhood robin which will follow every movement of your spade. Even much maligned moles take their toll of leatherjackets as well as other subterranean pests.

Many people regard the mole as a pest just because it occasionally leaves piles of soil on their pampered lawns. Often, after killing a mole, gardeners will go out and spend a fortune on John Innes No. 1, 2 or 3 without realising that the hills left by the mole are in fact superb sterilised compost which has cost them nothing. If only they were to stop and think they would see that moles are 'underground hedgehogs' with very similar habits, except that they never stop for a break from their hunting and never have time off for hibernation. They only construct their tunnel system once and, as only one mole would be resident on a lawn, the molehills would only occur infrequently during tunnel maintenance activity. One resident mole will fiercely prevent any other mole moving into a territory whereas an unoccupied lawn could attract a number, all raising molehills until tenancy is sorted out.

Strychnine and horrific break-back traps are the archaic solution to this animal's tunnelling. Many hedgehogs have lost legs and their lives in mole traps, dying slowly from blood loss and worse; and when they eat an earthworm laced with strychnine intended for a mole, or feed on a mole which has died of strychnine poisoning, their death throes are the cruellest form of torture imaginable. Many other creatures feed on dead earthworms and moles, once again passing on the strychnine legacy to the next generation of scavengers. As an alternative, why not try putting garlic cloves into mole tunnels or rotten fish, which are supposed to discourage them? Or, best of all, why not just collect the molehills – free from weed seeds it makes ideal potting compost – and leave the mole to go safely up and down its tunnel system collecting unwary underground bugs and grubs?

Badgers and of course birds also eat earthworms. They do not make any serious inroads into the worm population, fortunately because earthworms do a great deal of good, turning over and aerating the soil and burying enormous quantities of humus, the natural compost which has been supporting plant life for millions of years. Yet some gardening literature tells us that we need and can buy a worm killer, the reason for which is a mystery. The recommended poison is chlordane, one of the most persistent organo-chlorines which increase in potency the longer they are in the soil. Admittedly, worm casts can be a nuisance on bowling greens, but one bowler, playing on a chlordaned green in America, licked his fingers for a better grip on his woods and promptly died of poisoning.

Slugs are particularly resistant to organo-chlorines and when they browse on the corpses of poisoned worms the chlordane builds up in their bodies killing anything which preys on them, particularly hedgehogs. The dangers of chlordane are well known and it has been banned, along with other organo-chlorines, aldrin and dieldrin, as a spring seed dressing mainly because of the risk to birds, yet recently many herons have been found dead from dieldrin poisoning, which just shows how inefficient such limited restrictions are.

One major subject of contention is the hedgehogs' relationship with slugs which have grazed on slug pellets. Poisoning from slug pellets is real enough but is only the tip of the iceberg when it comes to destroying our wildlife. Slug pellets contain either metaldehyde or methiocarb, both potent poisons dangerous to animals and fish as well as to slugs. They are coloured blue and are supposed to taste nasty in order to deter birds and animals from eating them. Many cats and dogs have obviously not read the instructions and have been taken to vets after eating those nasty-tasting pellets. Blue is the favourite colour of many birds, and we have already seen, with the oil and blister beetles, that hedgehogs are not deterred by an unpleasant taste, though thankfully hedgehogs, like all other non-primate mammals, have predominantly black and white vision. All the same I believe that hedgehogs, especially youngsters, will pick up, lick and chew slug pellets especially as a stimulus to that peculiar hedgehog trait, self-lathering. Although it is supposed to take two thousand poisoned slugs to kill a hedgehog, even just a few may seriously debilitate it.

Scientists tell us that metaldehyde breaks down very quickly in dead slugs, but in a recent test no slugs dosed with the poison died within 24 hours and many did not die at all. Surely this means there are many slugs still alive containing small amounts of metaldehyde which can build up inside a predator.

We have had hedgehogs brought into St Tiggywinkles showing the classic symptoms of metaldehyde poisoning: extreme excitement and tremors with some stiffening of the muscles followed by partial paralysis. It is practically impossible to identify a poison in an animal but with hedgehogs one can usually assume they have had access to slug pellets, and when you hear that just 1 kilogram of slug pellets killed six calves you begin to realise how potent this poison is.

Read any of the health warnings on packets of insecticides: most of them warn 'keep away from fish, poultry and pets'. It's a pity they do not suggest keeping them away from wildlife. There is a whole army of pest-controllers working for you in the garden, with hedgehogs doing the bulk of the work. Interfere with their routines and you will be swamped with unwanted guests and will never again enjoy the evening company of the hedgehogs, shrews and their allies. In addition to the insecticides thrust upon us in gardening magazines and gardening centres there is a range of herbicides, just as toxic and as freely available. In fact one of them, paraquat, has no antidote and will kill if accidentally swallowed. There are methods of controlling weeds by organic means, but a little extra work in pulling them up can save expensive and needless poisoning.

Alix Lightfoot

The Nasties

The following few pages will make you itch, but please persevere and read them, as it is absolutely crucial to hedgehogs that their unwarranted reputation as carriers of fleas, and other parasites, is finally cleared up. Let's face it, they did not ask to be invaded with fleas, ticks and mites, so why should we make their burden worse by shunning them, maligning them and often mistreating and killing them?

Even when we do try to help them move their unwanted passengers with insecticidal preparations we sometimes end up killing not only the parasites but the hedgehog as well.

I had not planned to follow a chapter on the dangers of chemicals with another crusade, but I feel that I must try to outline some of the side effects of the products we are actively encouraged to spray, not just onto hedgehogs, but also on to our beloved cats and dogs. In the last chapter we saw that some chemicals on sale in gardening centres are suspected of causing cancer and genetic defects. Now I find that these are sold and even recommended for parasite control without even the warnings printed on the gardening products of a similar nature. Take a look at your cat or dog's flea spray and see how you

The notorious hedgehog flea will even infest young hedgehogs.

have subjected it, without realising it, to a dose of permethrin, carbaryl or gamma-BHC; or was it dichlorvos or fenitrothion which as well as being possible causes of cancer, and other problems, are registered as poisons. In fact these preparations operate as a mild nerve gas. While the Geneva Convention bans nerve gases in warfare, we are actively encouraged to subject animals to their effects. Sometimes parasites, particularly mange mites, are so firmly entrenched and debilitating that there is no alternative other than to resort to potent chemicals, but for the occasional inconvenient flea,

will you ever again dare put your pet's, or hedgehog's, life at risk by reaching for the aerosol spray? It's the same story – a broad-spectrum insecticide which kills everything it touches. Be more specific and ask your vet or pet shop for the mildest powder available to do a particular job and always, always keep strictly to the manufacturer's instructions.

Everybody knows that hedgehogs have fleas but just how many people realise that the hedgehog flea, *Archaeopsylla erinacei*, is a pest only to its spiky host and will not take a second look at a patch of inviting cat, dog or even human skin.

I want to tell you a story of an old lady who was forced to move out of the home she had known all her life into sheltered accommodation. Alone in her new strange home she had no friends and visitors but gradually five hedgehogs became regular and welcome callers to her back garden. Then all of a

sudden, with the coming of the warmer summer weather, her flat was invaded by hordes of fleas, jumping on her and biting her, causing an allergic reaction in her skin which warranted a visit to the doctor. In the old medical tradition he did not investigate the specific source of the fleas but resorted to the blanket answer: 'Get rid of the hedgehogs.' The poor lady's family joined in the pressure to stop her feeding her only regular visitors. Distraught and in tears she phoned St Tiggywinkles and we told her the truth – that hedgehog fleas will not infest a house and will certainly never cause the biting she was suffering. We asked her to get her doctor to contact us but to date we have heard nothing. Obviously the previous occupants had a cat or dog and the summer invasion was caused by the hatching of flea cocoons left behind in the carpet.

We have heard similar stories time and again, all

based on fallacies, but the accusations make people suspicious of hedgehogs. Fleas are certainly unwelcome, as much for their bites as for their disease-carrying capabilities. The difference between the hedgehog flea and the human, cat or dog flea is that the former will live only on hedgehogs; if it accidentally jumps onto another animal it will leave quickly. The other three fleas, together with the most sinister of all fleas, the rat flea, are far more promiscuous and do not mind on which animal they find their next meal – but not one has ever been found on a hedgehog. Since the hedgehog flea is specific to its host, there is also no danger of any disease which the flea may be carrying being transferred to you or your dog or cat.

If you are now convinced that hedgehog fleas pose no threat, I can tell you that on average a single animal may be host to a hundred fleas but I have personally counted over 1100, with many unaccounted for, on one hedgehog which had been cut free from a wire fence. Generally a hedgehog is unworried by its fleas but if the population becomes too high, it can become weakened by anaemia through loss of blood, so sometimes they do need some outside help in removing them. In the past they were sprayed with DDT or other chemical and not surprisingly died of poisoning once the fleas had gone. This gave rise to the belief that they could not live without them, to which of course the flourishing hedgehog population in New Zealand gives the lie. Another assumption, that because it could not groom itself fleas were necessary to stimulate the hedgehog skin, can be proved false by watching the contortions a hedgehog regularly performs to scratch every part of its body. Every now and then a good shake of all its spines rattles every one into its proper position.

With or without fleas the hedgehog plods on regardless, but when you are administering to an injured animal nothing is more disconcerting than to have fleas jump on you and then off. Even when they have gone you can sense them for hours afterwards. This, together with the fear of a flea spreading disease from a sick hedgehog to a fit one, makes their removal standard practice from any casualty which arrives at St Tiggywinkles (as long as the animal is not so seriously debilitated as to make any but the most necessary treatment dangerous).

We have had many casualties brought in which had been treated with the family cat or dog flea spray. Apart from their original problem they had the added burden of a dose of toxins which can be fatal or have long-lasting side effects. The golden rule should be to leave the fleas where they are but, if they must be removed, to use an insecticidal powder made from plant material: pyrethrum, which is quite harmless to mammals and birds, has no insidious effects. Johnson's Rid-Mite is a pyrethrum powder intended for use on pigeons and cage birds which are highly susceptible to anything stronger. We find it ideal for removing fleas from hedgehogs; in fact a good rule of thumb is that any animal powder bought from a pet shop for use on birds is generally safe for use on other animals.

Some commentators believe that hedgehogs have another method of flea control, that of self-lathering or *Selbstbespucken* ('spitting on oneself' in German). From a very early age some hedgehogs when confronted with something which gives off a strange odour will vigorously lick the substance, building up a mouthful of saliva. Then, performing the oddest contortions they will stretch over one shoulder and scatter foam, with the aid of their tongue, onto their spines. They were said to do this after chewing toad skins which helped combat their parasite load; but hedgehogs without parasites will do it as well as those with many. Another theory was that a strange scent – leather, tobacco, creosote or underfelt are just a few of the stimuli – increased the sexual attraction of the hedgehog; but, on the other hand, babies under two weeks old will self-lather at the slightest opportunity. In our nursery pens, when a newcomer is introduced, all the other babies will quickly gather round and lick the stranger then roll about all over the place trying to splatter saliva on to their own few spines.

Completely oblivious to its surroundings, a lathering hedgehog will perform for up to half an hour, but nobody knows why they do it. I believe it may be simply enjoying a pleasurable experience, rather like the family dog which always rolls in a cowpat the moment it is let off the lead.

In general, fleas do little harm to their hedgehog hosts but their habit of excreting blood amongst the spines can, in the summer, attract carrion-hunting blow flies whose larvae will literally eat the hedgehog alive if nothing is done to stop them. Many young or juvenile hedgehogs who have not quite mastered the art of nest-building will sleep out in the open during the day when flies are active. Consequently many are brought in to us suffering from myiasis, fly strike, although there are no obvious wounds. It is absolutely crucial that any hedgehog found in the summer months be checked over for fly eggs or maggots, both of which should be removed and killed without delay. In particular the greenbottle fly seems able to lay its eggs in the most inaccessible places. Obviously they will be clustered around wounds but other damp places are also attacked, noticeably the ears, eyes, nose, mouth and anus. The hairs on the face and along the fringes of the

A young hedgehog practises self-lathering.

The fly egg clusters that must be removed immediately.

body can become matted with eggs as do the warm damp places under the legs.

If there has been any delay in treating the hedgehog, some of the eggs may have hatched into miniature maggots immediately setting about their horrendous business of eating the hedgehog alive.

If you find a hedgehog in a similar condition or in any way injured and you lack the technical skills, equipment or even the stomach to tend to it, please help it by taking it to your vet – or ring our hedgehog hotline, Aylesbury 29860. You would probably have to pay for the veterinary treatment or for the casualty's transport to Aylesbury (see Chapter 10), but think of it as an investment in the future of our wildlife. However, you may find that some or all of the necessary treatment is within your capabilities, in which case you should read the following, and Chapters 9 and 10, carefully – some of it might even be useful to your vet, who, unlike ours, has probably had little or no occasion to treat a hedgehog. And don't forget, it's imperative that you always wash your hands after dealing with any injured or wild animal. Use a household disinfectant like Savlon or Dettol – but preferably a medical preparation like Hibiscrub.

The hedgehog tick, showing the eight legs of the arachnids.

Maggots Every individual egg and maggot must be laboriously removed with a pair of thin forceps or a pair of tweezers. A clear advantage can be gained by clipping away any facial or body hair containing eggs or maggots, with a miniature animal clipper; the model manufactured by Wahl is both small enough to get into the smaller crevices and rechargeable so that it can be used anywhere. Eggs or maggots in the mouth should be flushed out with a proprietary mouthwash, the eyes can be cleaned with clean warm water and the ears with a mild suspension of Savlon. After treatment the whole infected skin area should be dusted with Negasunt powder, made by Bayer, which will kill any maggots you may have missed. Both chemists and vets will carry Negasunt which also contains antibacterial agents suitable for wounds.

Sometimes maggots have penetrated deep into the hedgehog's body. Remove any that are near the surface then direct a hair dryer into the opening, making sure you do not burn the animal.

Maggots do not like a hot-dry environment and may evacuate the wound, allowing you to pick them off as they appear. Flushing with Savlon solution mixed with Negasunt can be just as effective if the Savlon is jetted deep into the wound from a syringe with a metal cannula attached.

Leaving Negasunt in the wound will catch any stragglers, although it must be cleaned out regularly. If there is a wound or any penetration of the skin then a course of antibiotics, which must be prescribed by a vet, should be started. It is important that the course is completed but, if the wound takes time to heal, the antibiotics may damage the gut flora essential for the digestion of the hedgehog's food. A meal of natural yoghurt after the treatment is finished will help restore the natural bacteria in the hedgehog's stomach. The antibiotic we have found most useful for this type of wound is amoxycillin. Only available from a veterinary surgeon who will confirm the dose rate and length of course as well as suggesting either injections or palatable drops that can be given by mouth.

To remove necrotic tissue (dead skin) and to encourage healing, the veterinary surgeon can supply Dermisol Multicleanse Solution (Beechams) which when applied liberally once

A typical cluster of ticks behind the ear.

similar to the adult and they do not go through the metamorphosis of a pupal stage. When they hatch from the egg the larvae look like small ticks but have only six legs instead of eight, making them very easy to confuse with insects.

The larva's only object in life is to obtain a meal of blood from some unsuspecting animal. Climbing a nearby grass stalk it waits to sense the approach of an animal, then stretches out and grasps the first of its hairs within reach. Once on board it quickly climbs to the bottom of the hair, sinks its hypostome – the bloodsucking tube between its jaws – into the animal's skin and gorges itself on blood.

The two species of tick found on hedgehogs, *Ixodes hexagonus* and *Ixodes ricinus*, the castor bean tick, are not removed by their hosts and, as with all parasites, are no problem until their numbers become too large for the hedgehog to cope with. It is estimated that about 70 ticks can kill a full grown rabbit in a week by taking so much blood as to make its host anaemic and weak. Hedgehogs are much smaller than rabbits so if they have many ticks it is important that they are removed as soon as possible. One juvenile hedgehog brought to us in a very weak state had 153 ticks embedded in its skin but when they were removed he quickly responded to recuperative treatment, mostly fluid therapy to replace liquids lost to the ticks.

Removing ticks is not as easy as it sounds; with that hypostome embedded in the skin there is the danger that the jaws may be broken off and left to fester. Insecticides have no effect on them so we bathe hedgehogs infested with ticks in a preparation called Alugan (Hoescht). It seems to incapacitate the ticks, enabling them to be cleanly lifted off with artery forceps. Grasping the tick close to the hedgehog's skin allows the hypostome to be pulled out cleanly. The tick sites should then be bathed with diluted Savlon and the removed ticks doused in a dish of surgical spirit. You will often miss the minute unfed adults but often, overnight, they will take their meal of blood and appear as the grey-blue pea-shaped lumps which show they are ready to drop off the hedgehog to continue the tick cycle.

On hedgehogs, ticks are usually found clustered behind and in the ears; those unfed adults which always congregate around the base of the tail never seem to grow – perhaps the hedgehog makes a meal of them when it is curled up in a ball.

or twice a day, is remarkably effective. Dermisol is expensive but is absolutely essential if the wound is to heal with the minimum possible delay.

Sometimes the maggot infestation is so severe and so far advanced into the body that there is no hope of saving the animal from a very nasty death. In cases like this your veterinary surgeon should be asked to put the unfortunate hedgehog to sleep painlessly. But don't give up too soon: hedgehogs are remarkably resilient and can often overcome the most severe problems.

Lice Many other animal species and most birds are infested with the well-known parasitic insect, the louse. However *I have not come across any lice on the many hedgehogs which pass through St Tiggywinkles.* Unfortunately the same is not true of the parasitic member of the spider family, the *Acarinae*, ticks and mange mites.

Ticks Ticks are the heavyweights of the parasites, they are the greyish-blue balloon-like lumps found clinging to so many hedgehogs. Unlike many insects their larval form looks very

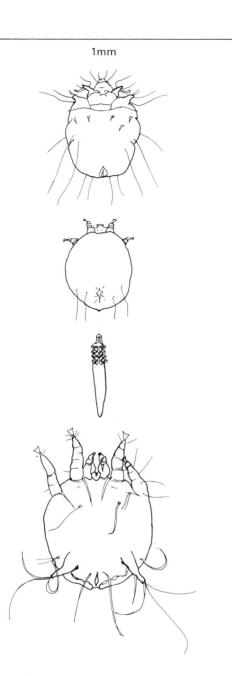

1mm

The four species of mite that have been found on hedgehogs.

Mites The other parasitic members of the *Acarinae* are much harder to detect than ticks, many of them being visible only through a microscope. However, small as they are, mites manage to cause serious problems to hedgehogs, including anaemia, weakness and, in severe cases, death.

The only mite clearly visible to the naked eye is the hedgehog mange mite *Caparinia tripilis* which we find on about 10 per cent of the hedgehogs brought in to us. As you handle the hedgehog it is possible to see the mites running up and down the body hairs: they are the small mobile dots as opposed to the much larger fleas. In Germany and New Zealand this mange mite is responsible for many hedgehog deaths: victims are seen to get weaker and lie on their side unable to roll up. Often the eyes are obstructed and the animal loses all sense of day or night and eventually sinks into a hypothermic torpor just prior to death.

Again, treatment is a warm bath in Alugan, at the manufacturer's strongest recommended solution. As the hedgehog is totally immersed it will open and try to escape the bowl. Then is the time, using a 10 ml syringe, to squirt Alugan down into its spines. Do not dry the hedgehog with a towel but let it drip dry under a ceramic heater. A 100 watt heater suspended twelve inches above the hedgehog is sufficient but the animal must be able to move away from the heat if it becomes uncomfortable. Repeat the bath after ten days to destroy any mites that may have escaped the first treatment.

Sarcoptic mange is caused by the mite burrowing into the hedgehog's skin and causing hair and spines to fall out. The skin becomes damaged and open to infection and gradually the hedgehog can become emaciated and eventually die of exhaustion. The mange usually starts on the face and nose but quickly spreads to the rest of the body. One recent television series on hedgehogs followed the movement of one animal which obviously had a mite infestation. As it progressed, the infestation could be seen growing to horrible proportions. For some reason veterinary literature in Britain plays down and even denies the existence of mange in hedgehogs, so this TV star had to go on suffering regardless.

As with *Caparinia tripilis*, sarcoptic mange can be cleared with Alugan baths although a heavy build-up of scabby material may need more drastic treatment: ease the scabs off with forceps

95

Mange mites are the principal cause of skin disorders but after treatment the spines grow back.

or tweezers then dab the area every two days with Temadex ointment from Wellcome.

Mite infestation of a hedgehog's ears can cause inflammation, disorientation and fits. Treatment can involve drops to kill mites deep in the ear and the inevitable Alugan baths for those outside the ear.

We have had one suspected case of Demodectic mange where mites live in the hair follicles causing spines to fall out. The hedgehog we suspected of suffering from this problem unfortunately died before we could institute treatment. Probably Alugan would not affect the *Demodex* mite, but Temadex ointment has apparently proved effective on other animals.

Another common form of mange we have encountered in hedgehogs leaves a dusty deposit on the hairs especially around the face. As yet we have not been able to identify the species of mite, but we have found Alugan useful in destroying it.

Ringworm In New Zealand the mite *Caparinia tripilis* apparently opened up the skin for invasion by the hedgehog ringworm, *Trichophyton erinacei*, a fungus which forms patches of dry, crusty skin with bald patches where the hair has fallen out. Ringworm is highly contagious and may be transferred to man but appears to be rare in hedgehogs. At St Tiggywinkles we have had a very few cases of ringworm, certainly nothing like the 20 per cent suggested in some publications. If it occurs in a hedgehog, griseofulvin sprinkled on its food should prove effective. Ringworm may occasionally give a human contact slight dermatitis but this should clear up within about a week.

Worms So far we have only been concerned with the ectoparasite which we can see but by far the most damaging to hedgehogs are the endo-parasites, those insidious nematode and cestode worms which lurk in the animal's vital organs. Often a population of endo-parasites is able to live comfortably within its host without causing any problems. However, if the animal is slightly under the weather or host to other parasites, the balance is disturbed and the hedgehog can die from emaciation.

By far the most prolific of the worms affecting hedgehogs are the nematodes which live in its lungs, oesophagus and intestines. Recent research suggests that rather than picking up the infestation many baby hedgehogs are born with these parasites. The most debilitating are the lungworms, *Crenosoma striatum* and *Capillaria aerophila*, which are responsible for the deaths of infant as well as adult hedgehogs. Symptoms of their presence include a horrid rattling cough but sometimes even babies show no symptoms. The damage they do to lung tissues brings on broncho-pneumonia, eventually killing the hedgehog.

It should be standard practice for every hedgehog in care to be routinely dosed with an anthelmintic: we now dose every inmate with Panacur Paste which contains fenbendazole. One problem arose in that Panacur is in a syringe intended for horses, a little large for a hedgehog; but by filling a 1 ml syringe with a blunted 16 g needle attached, we can measure small doses, about 0.05 ml direct onto the hedgehog's tongue. The treatment should be repeated twice at fortnightly intervals.

This initial dosing with Panacur should also clear any oesophageal worms, *Physaloptera clausa* and intestinal *Capillaria*. *Physaloptera* may grow quite large but generally do not cause any problems, whereas *Capillaria* can build up in the intestines and cause chronic enteritis (see pp.125–6).

By far the largest internal parasite you are likely to encounter in a hedgehog is its very own tapeworm, *Hymenolepis erinacei*, identified from a stool sample. Treatment is with praziquantel 10–15 mg by mouth or niclosamide 200 mg per kilogram of bodyweight (Droncit or Yomesan).

Diseases Very little is known about any specific diseases which hedgehogs might harbour. Forty per cent of rats carry the bacteria of leptospirosis, the yellow jaundice which causes Weill's disease in man, and although hedgehogs can apparently suffer from the disease we have found no evidence amongst the casualties brought in. It is said that an adult hedgehog is an equal match in a fight with a rat, so possibly these recorded cases of leptospirosis were after such an encounter. **Any hedgehogs picked up which have a yellowing of the mucous membranes in the mouth should be isolated and referred to a veterinary surgeon. The disease is highly contagious so every hygienic precaution should be taken including wearing rubber gloves when handling the infected animal and of course washing the hands afterwards.** With their often dirty eating habits hedgehogs, especially in captivity, occasionally pick up Salmonella bacteria, which can be identified in the droppings. As with any diarrhoeal infection, strict hygiene should be observed, including sterilising feed bowls in Milton between feeds. After confirmation of an infection and sensitivity to tests the veterinary surgeon will be able to prescribe a suitable treatment. Chloromycetin succinate has been successful but extreme care should be taken as the use of chloramphenicol is highly restricted – hopefully sensitivity tests will suggest a more suitable antibiotic.

Although Salmonella enteritidis seems to thrive in captive hedgehogs it does not cause any known problems to wild animals. Bordetella bronchiseptica is another bacteria like this which thrives when hedgehogs are kept together and causes lung infections. Often associated with lungworm infestation it should respond to antibiotics especially oxytetracycline at 50 mg per kilogram of bodyweight each day. We have found that practically all hedgehogs have a touch of pneumonia in the wild: often when they are brought into a confined condition it seems to flare up and cause breathing problems. It's as well for a vet to treat any hedgehog suffering from lung problems with antibiotics as well as anthelmintics.

Research has shown that hedgehogs can carry rabies. But even in countries where rabies exists – unlike Britain – hedgehogs, because they are at ground level and rarely bite anyway, would not pose much of a threat unless one were regularly handling them. Another point in their favour is that they do not appear to become infected with bovine tuberculosis which has had such a dramatic effect on man's relationship with badgers. One hedgehog, out of many, was found to be suffering from avian tuberculosis but this would never be a threat to cattle or man. Hedgehogs are resistant to many diseases but, along with the armadillo, have the dubious privilege of being highly susceptible to leprosy in the warm parts of the world. No doubt if animals are needed for research into the disease then poor old hedgehogs, being more numerous than armadillos, will be selected.

There are no recorded cases of hedgehogs passing any disease, other than those supposed cases of ringworm, on to man or his cats, dogs and livestock, so if strict conditions of hygiene are observed during any encounters there should be no ill effects from dealings with hedgehogs. *But, if in doubt, always refer any queries to a veterinary surgeon.*

Amy Williams

In Defence of Hedgehogs

by Pam Ayres

I am very fond of hedgehogs
Which makes me want to say
That I am struck with wonder
How there's any left today.
For each morning as I travel,
And no short distance that,
All I see are hedgehogs,
Squashed. And dead. And flat.

Now, hedgehogs are not clever,
No, hedgehogs are quite dim,
And when he sees your headlamps,
Well it don't occur to him
That the very wisest thing to do
Is up and run away.
No, he curls up in a stupid ball
And no doubt starts to pray.

Well motor cars do travel
At a most alarming rate,
And by the time you sees him,
It is very much too late.
And thus he gets a-squasho'd,
Unrecorded but for me,
With me pen and paper,
Sittin' in a tree.

It is statistically proven,
In chapter and in verse,
That in a car-and-hedgehog fight,
The hedgehog comes off worse.
When whistlin' down your prop shaft,
And bouncin' off your diff,
His coat of nice brown prickles
Is not effect-iff.

A hedgehog cannot make you laugh,
Whistle, dance or sing,
And he ain't much to look at,
And he don't make anything,
And in amongst his prickles,
There's fleas and bugs and that,
But there ain't no need to leave him
Squashed. And dead. And flat.

Oh, spare a thought for hedgehogs,
Spare a thought for me,
Spare a thought for hedgehogs,
As you drink your cup of tea,
Spare a thought for hedgehogs,
Hoverin' on the brinkt,
Spare a thought for hedgehogs,
Lest they become extinct.

'Once you get to the white line you're safe.'

Danger!

MAN IS generally not adversely affected by the presence of hedgehogs. I wish I could say the same about the effect of man's presence on the hedgehog. Everywhere the hedgehog wanders on his nightly forays it meets man and his paraphernalia: dogs, plastic bags, ice cream cartons and, of course, his motor cars.

It has often been suggested that the only sure way of establishing an accurate census of hedgehogs is to count the number of corpses left behind by hit and run drivers. Sadly those pathetic little corpses left behind are an important indicator of hedgehog mortality and show that many thousands of them die on the roads or drag themselves off, crippled, to die under some damp cold hedge.

They venture out onto the hostile carriageways to feast on the insects which gather on the warm tarmac or to feed on the carrion left by other hit and run drivers or just to cross the road. Most motorists manage to avoid a rock or other obstacle lying in their path so why is it that so many do not take evasive action when confronted by an immobile animal? A moving animal may be very difficult to avoid: it's practically impossible to miss a squirrel which materialises out of the darkness, but a hedge-hog, sensing the approach of No. 1 enemy, will freeze, tucking its face under the futile protection of its spiky forehead. I feel sure that in some cases safe evasive action could have been taken; the sad truth seems to be that many motorists don't care.

The remains of a hedgehog on the road last for a long time, whereas other animal carcasses are soon cleared up by crows and scavengers. There have been surveys of these long-lasting reminders, not to try to establish population censuses but to try to measure the extent of the carnage. I think we all know that hedgehogs and rabbits are the principal victims but the figure of 60 per cent of all road casualties strikes a chill when you realise that hedgehogs do not have the reproductive capacities of rabbits. The percentage killed is apparent from all the published surveys, but unfortunately these seem to disagree on other aspects of hedgehog mortality. In Britain one survey suggests that the worst period on the road is during April and May when the hedgehogs are newly risen from hibernation, while another states that the height of the breeding season, July and August, are the months when hedgehogs are most vulnerable with more males being hit in the earlier months and females not venturing forth until the autumn, after the peak

Over 2 million hedgehogs are killed yearly on the world's roads – but chemicals are their main killers.

period. I must add that in the earlier months of the hedgehog year we are inundated with male casualties and have hardly any females. German hedgehogs, apparently, have two peak periods of roadside activity, in June and October, with a survey also revealing that on one 150 kilometre stretch of autobahn there was one hedgehog killed annually on each kilometre of carriageway as compared with one every 12 miles (around 20 kilometres) on the quieter roads of Norfolk during 1960. Before so many households had a car, in 1952, 1953 and 1954 a survey in Hampshire showed that only between one and three hedgehogs were killed on each 100 miles (160 kilometres) of road.

Now that the two-car family is the norm I can only assume that the present figures are even more horrific. It is not hard to see that the estimated hedgehog road mortality toll in Denmark of between 70,000 and 100,000 each year is probably true for all European countries, with the figures adjusted depending on how many miles of road (there are about 200,000 miles – 320,000 kilometres – in Britain alone) and how many cars per head there are in any country. In New Zealand, where hedgehog densities are thought to be greater, the road casualty rate is even higher than in Europe, so world-wide figures of hedgehogs killed annually on the roads must be in the region of two to three million. No wonder people frequently say to me now that they do not see hedgehogs, not even dead ones, any more.

In Britain I think we can estimate that in any year at least 100,000 hedgehogs are killed on the roads. When, recently, 80 members of the Mammal Society surveyed 7846 mammal corpses and found that 2746 of them were hedgehogs, warning bells of 'endangered species' started to ring.

Surprisingly, the Mammal Society also found out that hedgehogs do not seem to have a high mortality rate on the newer high-speed motorways and dual carriageways where only 5 per cent of their corpses were found. However, 16 per cent were on quiet B roads, 28 per cent on unclassified and 56 per cent on the A roads which unfortunately make up the majority of Britain's highways network.

In well-lit urban areas where there are speed limits you would expect motorists to be able to avoid the occasional hedgehog. But 35 per cent of the casualties were found in these areas; not much less than the 48 per cent found on unlit country roads near to farms and farm buildings, where another man-made hazard accidentally takes its toll of wildlife. Cattle grids are ideal for keeping livestock in ungated fields, deer in their parks and ponies safely off the main roads, but many other animals try to cross them, often with disastrous results. There was the obstreperous old crow which had broken several feathers trying to fly out through the bars, there have been baby rabbits who thought the dark recesses were an inviting burrow and of course the inevitable hedgehog which has tumbled in to sniff out the insects and carrion hidden in the gloom. Hedgehogs and crows are able to exist for a while on any creature unfortunate enough to fall into the pit but in their efforts to escape from their dungeon they themselves eventually succumb to exhaustion and starvation. A campaign has now started to encourage designers of cattle grids to install ramps so that any animal with enough sense can climb out of its prison. The ramp can be concrete or wood but

If you find an occupied nest, do not touch anything but immediately re-cover the family.

must be 20 centimetres wide and not inclined at more than 30 degrees; and, since most cattle grids have a central wall dividing the well, two ramps should be fitted or a 10 centimetre gap left under the wall.

Unfortunately hedgehogs seem to be attracted to those dark, dank places which every other animal likes to avoid. Leave a drain uncovered and a hedgehog will climb into it, only to find that it cannot get out. If it is lucky enough to be spotted, it can usually be removed without too much bother. However, one hedgehog to whose rescue I was called at a local primary school had fallen so snugly into a drain that it was impossible to slide anything underneath the animal to lift it clear. With an audience of anxious schoolchildren I had to come up with an answer. Then I remembered that it was supposedly possible to lift a hedgehog with just one of its spines. In the tool box of my car (this was before B P had donated the new vehicle which does not need a constant tool kit) was a very stout, if oily, pair of pliers. I had no alternative so I gripped the nearest spine, pulled gently and, to a rousing cheer from the audience, lifted the hedgehog clear. Of course I told the schoolchildren not to try to do the same themselves but, although I hated the thought of having to try it again, there is now a brand-new pair of pliers in my animal emergency kit, just in case. Luckily, most drains in people's gardens are covered but a great many hedgehogs must perish in the drains at the sides of country roads.

The hedgehog's fondness for dark, tight holes is always getting it into trouble, but no holes are more sinister than the inviting lengths of pipe put down by gamekeepers to lure the stoat and weasel which are, apart from the fox, the most maligned of British fauna. Hunting rats or mice they go into the tunnels lured by a tantalising bait – and the same thing happens to hedgehogs. The last thing they hear is the 'click' as the trap breaks their back.

Thankfully gamekeepers are becoming an endangered species but many hedgehogs are killed by accident because of the lack of a modicum of foresight on the part of ordinary people. Take the garden pond for instance: an oasis for wildlife, somewhere for the birds to drink or the frogs to breed, but a death-trap for a thirsty hedgehog which falls in and cannot climb the steep plastic sides. It can swim well but after hours of desperate circling it will finally succumb and drown. A sloping bank or stairway of rocks or even a piece of chickenwire dangling over the edge might have been its salvation. A swimming pool is just a pond on a larger scale and there is no escape for the hapless mouse, frog, bird or even hedgehog which happens to fall in. A floating wooden ledge anchored in one corner would be a safe haven until rescue arrived or perhaps someone should incorporate an escape ramp into swimming pool design?

Most gardens are not lucky enough to have a swimming pool but many have compost heaps, great favourites with hedgehogs as nest sites. A compost heap may appear harmless enough but when it's time to spread it on the garden, how many gardeners check it before that first thrust of the fork? I would hate to tell you how many gardeners have heard the scream of a mother hedgehog and her babies as he spears not just one but two or three of them on the tines of his fork. Naturally many hedgehogs are killed in this way, although we treat many dozens

Hedgehogs are good swimmers but will drown if they can't climb out of ponds or swimming pools.

which white-faced gardeners have managed to rescue. I believe that composting is a crucial part of non-chemical gardening so I would hate to see gardeners curbing the practice. Checking the heap before the first thrust of the fork may save a hedgehog and her family; a wait of only a few weeks will then give them time to grow and go their own way.

It's not only hedgehogs which nest in compost heaps: bank voles and long-legged wood mice have their minute babies in its warmth and there is always the chance, if you are lucky, that the harmless grass snake may find it suitable for egg-laying and incubation.

Other piles of garden refuse may prove to be even more lethally attractive to hedgehogs: heaps of faggots or old twigs or, as Cinders one of our patients preferred, just plain dried leaves have all been death-traps because they were all potential bonfires. Cinders was lucky that the people setting fire to her pile of leaves heard her screams before she was permanently injured. Normally hedgehogs caught in bonfires are blinded, but all Cinders lost was a batch of spines off her back. She has now recovered and been released, although with a clump of spines shorter than the others.

Every heap of leaves, twigs or rubbish that is destined to become a bonfire should be turned over completely just before lighting, and especially early in the year, the upper parts should be checked in case a thrush, blackbird or robin has decided to nest in this man-made thicket. November 5th, Guy Fawkes' night, takes its toll of hedgehogs so, even if the bonfire is to be enormous, try to make sure that no animal has made its way in underneath what will soon be an inferno.

They say that accidents are more likely to happen in the home but with hedgehogs it is in the garden that a moment's lapse of concentration by the gardener could result in a hedgehog in the long grass being scalped by the mower or having its nose sliced off with a strimmer. Hedgehogs make a habit of getting trapped in the plastic bean netting, twisting and turning until they nearly sever a leg or seriously damage their throats. Start pea and bean netting at least 30 centimetres off the ground and, please, resist the black cotton which does not scare the birds off seed beds but collects all manner of severed limbs, and hedgehogs. Wire netting is just as bad; and I have ruined many cricket and tennis nets by having to cut hedgehogs free. These nets are often left lying on the ground when not in use, an open invitation for any hedgehog looking for a cosy nest site.

While you are not looking, a hedgehog will sneak into your garage and try to drown itself in that tray of old sump oil you have not got around to throwing away. If you have a pit, a hedgehog will fall down it; one was even seen licking the corrosion on an old car battery. Anti-freeze is apparently highly palatable even though poisonous. Hedgehogs have a fascination for rings: the end cut off a plastic pipe makes a lethal collar and young hedgehogs will even squeeze into key rings. A juvenile I treated recently was a peculiar shape, waisted like a wasp. When I looked closely I discovered that as a baby he must have crawled through a key ring and then grown round it with the result that he was nearly cut in half. Along with the pliers in my emergency kit I now have a pair of powerful side-cutting tin-snips for cutting hedgehogs free. Remember, if there is a hazard in the garden, a hedgehog is bound to find it.

The four plastic rings used to hold cans of beer are another hazard for wildlife. Look around any lay-by or picnic site and you will see the empty yoghurt or ice cream cartons in which a hedgehog

The hedgehog and the tortoise – both well protected from the enemy.

can get its head stuck; or the broken glass which can cut its very soft underbelly; and there are plastic bags to suffocate it and ring pulls which can sever a foot or nose. No wonder the Keep Britain Tidy Group adopted Spikey the Hedgehog as a mascot for their 'Take Your Litter Home' campaign. Now that there are fewer litter bins to attract wildlife I hope that more people respect the signs and take their rubbish home. I would be very relieved if I never had to cut another hedgehog free from a piece of man's discarded rubbish.

As I see it, most of these hazards can be overcome with a little thought, but unfortunately I can see no way of preventing the inquisitive dog from injuring itself and on occasion a hedgehog. Many dogs love to snuffle in and out of the undergrowth, and a hedgehog is an exciting scent. Although some dogs will just stand and bark, others, even the most mild-tempered, will make a grab for the hedgehog. Many hedgehogs end up with blood on their spines but a careful check reveals no wounds: another dog has learned its lesson. However, some hedgehogs are not so lucky and suffer dog bite wounds which invariably become infected; but once the wound is cleaned in dilute Savlon and the vet has prescribed a course of antibiotics, the hedgehog will usually recover and can be released.

Although dogs will not generally eat hedgehogs, in the past they were of course a favourite dish of gypsies. I thought the practice had died out until I read a recent letter in the Hedgehog Preservation Society newsletter. The correspondent described how, in the First World War, she had regularly eaten roasted hedgehog, tasting not unlike pork. She wanted to know if modelling clay was any good for roasting hedgehogs in and if there were any recipes available. Apparently the writer still had hedgehog traps which she could use as her sister thought poison might taint the food. Incidentally the writer also wanted to know of any ways of preserving her victims as she did not own a 'deep freeze machine'.

This type of thinking is rare which is fortunate since hedgehogs, in spite of their generous defences, still have to face many natural predators which catch and eat them to survive. But there's an old proverb which says reassuringly, 'The fox has many tricks, the hedgehog only one and that greater than them all.' Foxes do take a few hedgehogs but even in winter when food is scarce and foxes can dig out hibernation nests they make up only 3 per cent of the foxes' total diet. Foxes appear to have an aversion to

insectivores; perhaps many, like shrews, have an unpleasant taste.

Badgers are quite capable of forcing a hedgehog open with their powerful front claws or simply of biting through the coat of spines. Hedgehogs seem to know this and when they meet a badger will not roll up but will tuck their heads in and scream piteously. I once removed a hedgehog whose screams had attracted me from some distance away. The badger had fled but the hedgehog continued screaming and as I bent down to pick it up, it bucked its head forwards, presumably using its spines to try to fight off the badger. However, not all hedgehogs escape: an empty hedgehog skin turned inside out means that a badger has found a good meal.

Polecats, ancestors of the domestic ferret and now rare in Britain, are related to badgers in the tribe of carnivorous *Mustelidae* but, unlike their cousins, will eat every scrap of the hedgehog – flesh, bones, bristles and spines. Presumably mink and otters take their toll of hedgehogs, but no evidence has been found of the smaller *Mustelidae*, the stoat and weasel, breaching the spiny defence.

An adult hedgehog can protect itself against rats, although these often take youngsters from nests and have the underhand habit of preying on adult hedgehogs when they are deep in hibernation and unable to defend themselves. The domestic and feral cats, however, do not pose any problems to hedgehogs; in fact they appear to live side by side, often sharing the same food bowl.

In Europe, wild boar have been seen eating everything in sight including hedgehogs; and presumably in Africa and Asia the larger carnivorous cats will not hesitate to add a passing hedgehog to their menu. It is known that in Africa the four-toed hedgehog is the favourite prey of the enormous Verraux'

Eagle Owl, *Bubo lacteus*, whose giant talons and beak have no trouble penetrating the hedgehog's spiny armour. Europe's owls and larger birds of prey do not have the same power and of 102,000 food pellets checked for content, only 134, 0.1 per cent, were found to contain hedgehog remains.

The only birds which are a regular threat to hedgehogs are the opportunist magpies which will not hesitate to mob any hedgehog out during the day, pecking it into submission by attacking its vulnerable head and eyes.

Most other wild animals and birds respect the hedgehog's defences but even in New Zealand, where there are no carnivorous mammals, the weka, a rail-like bird, has been seen walking off with a young hedgehog in its mouth. One report of how the American puma seizes a hedgehog by the head and gradually draws the animal through its teeth, peeling off the skin, seems doubtful as there are no hedgehogs for the puma to meet in the Americas.

Hedgehogs are most vulnerable when they are in hibernation and the choice of nest site is crucial. If it is too low-lying, the hedgehog may be drowned in an overnight winter flood. Nesting in a hedge may result in the hedgehog being mangled by the monstrous machines farmers use to enlarge their fields or burned when the stubble is cleared.

All told, the hedgehog has survived against natural predation for millions of years. Man has now stacked the odds against it, yet if we are a little more vigilant we can make sure that there will still be hedgehogs for our children to enjoy.

Sarah Bryan

Hedgehog Aid: the Action

(with Hedgehog First Aid)

ALTHOUGH IT was nearly twenty years ago I still have not managed to wipe out the vivid memory of the unfortunate hedgehog I found in London, fighting its losing battle against injury.

In the busy years which followed that encounter I had very little opportunity to make contact with other birds and animals. My ten years in an accountant's office at Earl's Court had trained me in all the facets of business life enabling me, in 1970, shortly after my son Colin was born, to take the plunge and leave London to set up my own refrigeration company in the fresh air of Aylesbury.

From then on every hour was taken up with business. The terrible irony was that whenever I did manage to flee the office for the countryside I was always hurrying to and from appointments and only ever saw fleeting glimpses of wildlife in my rearview mirror or as pathetic squashed messages on the roads.

Regularly I travelled the length and breadth of England and Wales never having time to pause and appreciate the greenery but always finding a moment to stop and investigate those little bundles which seemed to cry out to me from the kerbs and hard shoulders: they might still be alive, there was always the chance. Whether it meant turning in muddy farm gateways, reversing up motorways or stopping in the middle of traffic, every bundle had to be turned over. I have sprinted across carriageways to rescue bundles of rags, been drenched by passing cars as I investigated paper bags and clambered through ditches to rescue pieces of tyre that looked like injured badgers. But every genuine casualty was beyond help. There was one thing I did find out: there are ghouls who will endanger their own lives – not to save an animal but by stopping even on a motorway to cut the tail off a fox left lying there by a hit and run driver. I always stopped for those foxes, simply to give them a more dignified resting place under a hedge or bush.

It was always the same story: I would drive as fast as I could to an appointment to buy refrigeration spares or do a deal on a quantity of frozen food, then return even faster to the factory with its bottomless piles of paperwork, returns and bills. Did I really need to give up my life for money? After all, it only seemed to evaporate on an endless round of parties, new cars and outdoing the Joneses. What would I look back on if the ulcers and heart disease ever let me reach retirement? Quite honestly, not much, I began to think. I seemed to see less and less of Sue. Colin was becoming a stranger as he grew up. Poor lad, he had plenty of toys but his playground was the factory. I never had time to sit him on my knee before the telephone would ring with my next itinerary.

I know that all three of us wanted me to leave the rat-race and one dank November night as we snatched a few days' holiday in the only hotel open in Ilfracombe we made the fateful decision. It was Guy Fawkes' night as we walked the deserted Devon streets. With us were Julie, the pet spaniel which we'd had to smuggle in and out of the hotel room, and Purdie, the rescued kestrel who had to sleep in the car. We could hardly wait until morning to get home and start the wheels rolling. At first light we paid our bill and set off like bats out of hell back to civilisation to tell everybody of our great decision.

Before long we had managed to sell our business, for a pittance but at least it gave me a year in which to try to find a way into the world of wildlife conservation through the back door – by writing articles for magazines. If I did not succeed during that year, we would have to think again.

My deadline was creeping nearer when, instead of the usual flood of rejection slips, there was an acceptance – an article on snakes for a wildlife magazine. Suddenly I had a boost of confidence, but without all those rejection slips how would I finish papering the walls of my study?

That was ten years ago. My articles were being accepted and at last I had an excuse to go out into the woods and fields to watch my subjects. We spent two months excavating an ichthyosaur we had found, we watched fox cubs gambolling in the warm sunshine and walked mile after unhurried mile searching the ploughed fields for bygone artefacts to build up a picture of life as it had been. My favourite indulgence became walking and driving the empty lanes at 5.30 each evening imagining and remembering the mayhem at Hyde Park Corner.

I had more time to concentrate on Purdie in her aviary. Then a tawny owl with a torn wing arrived, followed by a wood pigeon and a one-eyed kestrel I plucked from the hard shoulder of the M40 on one of my rare trips to London.

The word soon got out that at last here was someone to whom people could take the injured birds and animals which have become such a part of daily life. Soon sparrows, blackbirds, starlings and birds of all shapes and sizes were filling my growing collection of aviaries.

I took the opportunity, in between writing articles, to visit every secondhand book store I could trace, searching for any reference to wildlife care. I discovered that virtually nothing had been written on the subject. I gathered what I could and avidly read every word, two or three times. However, much of the information was of little use and working alongside my local vet I had to learn most of the techniques, especially where birds were concerned, from experience and the application of common sense. We started to have our successes but the more animals and birds we released, the more seemed to arrive, until inevitably another hedgehog, just clinging to life and reminiscent of that one in London, arrived on my doorstep.

The only difference between the two was that this hedgehog actively resisted my help. The only indication of distress was a leg poking out of the centre of an impregnable spiky ball. The animal was obviously still strong but something did not smell right; instead of the usual muddy scent of an animal which lives by rooting around in the leaf litter under hedges, there was the distinct odour of decay. I had met this smell before on other bird and animal casualties, it was the sign of severe infection, an old wound that if not treated would lead to septicemia, the blood poisoning which is nearly always fatal.

How on earth could I possibly persuade the hedgehog to unroll in order to trace the source of infection? The more I tried to force the prickly ball open, the tighter it seemed to roll, flexing its spines so that my hands were starting to smart with the constant stabbing. Somehow, the other hedgehog had not seemed as prickly as this, but it had been much weaker and probably unable to flex its spines. Then I had a brainwave: if I dripped warm water into the tiny gap where I could just see its nose, the hedgehog would have to unroll. But, no, the water seemed to find some unseen channel and run out all over the table. I had always found, when working with bird casualties, that the gentle approach was often more successful so I started to stroke those vicious spines and there was some response but after half an hour, with very sore hands, I decided that I was getting nowhere. I would have to come up with another solution.

When I had first started working with injured birds I had read that it was quite simple to anaesthetise them with a pad of cottonwool soaked in ether. I had bought a bottle but decided against using it because I was concerned that it might adversely affect a bird's respiratory system, invading the air sacs which could hold remnants of ether even after the bird had recovered. Also, ether is highly volatile especially in the confines of my small medical room. Ever since, the tightly stoppered bottle had sat in the cupboard, unused. This hedgehog definitely needed urgent attention. There was nothing else I could do – I would have to resort to the ether.

Even if the anaesthetic worked I would not have much time before the hedgehog came round and once more rolled back into an obstinate ball, so I made sure everything I needed was close at hand before I started. A kidney dish of warm water slightly coloured with Savlon, a cetrimide disinfectant; a heap of cottonwool balls; a pair of forceps and a sharp pair of scissors just in case there was wire netting or string wrapped around the leg. Opening all the windows to let the gas escape I poured some of the ether over a wad of cottonwool inside a jar and closed the lid.

With everything ready, I laid Hannibal, as we later christened him, on the table, injured leg sticking upwards, and applied the cold wad of soaked cottonwool to the gap above where his nose would be. The reaction was almost instantaneous. The prickly ball was transformed into a very active hedgehog, which sped off across the table dragging the injured leg behind him – through the pile of cottonwool balls, over the dish of Savlon, tipping it up in the process, and nearly off the edge of the table before I managed to stop him. When I got him back to the centre of the table, he had once again become that prickly ball with a leg sticking out, but this time festooned with Savlon-soaked cottonwool balls. Fifteen-love to the hedgehog.

'You're very prickly today.'

Re-organising the table I soaked another wad of cottonwool in ether and applied it to Hannibal. This time I was ready for the break for freedom, but when it came and I tried to hold him his spines were so painful that I had to let go – another dish of Savlon all over the table. Thirty-love to the hedgehog.

By this time the smell of ether was, I am sure, beginning to affect me but I now had the measure of the hedgehog and donning a pair of leather gloves I once more applied the soporific. Hannibal was waiting and sprang open almost immediately, but this time I grabbed the animal with my gloved left hand and firmly, but gently, put the pad of ether over his nose. He bucked, bit, rolled and generally tried to throw me off but gradually he slowed down and finally went completely limp.

Game, set and match to the ether.

Quickly disposing of the pad I turned Hannibal on to his back in order to look at the injured leg and promptly dislodged a mass of anaesthetised fleas. Ignoring them I finally managed to look at the leg and, as I expected, found a horribly infected wound which smelt awful and oozed pus into the now matted underbody hair.

Gingerly I moved the swollen leg up and down, back and forth but happily could not feel any crepitus, where two pieces of broken bone grate together, so I knew we did not have the problem of a compound infected fracture which would probably not heal. No, all we had here was an old wound, possibly caused by a bite or thorn, which had become infected. Using the cottonwool balls soaked in Savlon solution I firmly set about cleaning all the matter from inside the wound. If it was not completely clear, it would never start to heal. Using each piece of cottonwool only once to prevent the infection being spread, I irrigated the wound with a 10 cm cannula fitted to a 10 ml syringe to get the warm Savlon into even the deepest parts of the wound cavity, dislodging and flushing out any obstinate particles which could impair the healing process. An abscess like this will continue filling with matter so should not be closed with a dressing, sutures or just ointment; in fact some abscesses have to be surgically opened to allow them to drain but that is strictly the domain of the veterinary surgeon.

Satisfied that the wound was as clean as possible I quickly sponged the underfur – just in time, as the animal came round, contorted himself to turn on his stomach and once again headed straight for the Savlon dish. His complement of fleas were also coming back to life, crawling drunkenly in all directions, though none of them were yet conscious enough to be able to jump back onto Hannibal. I swept them all up before they had the chance.

I would need to go through this rigmarole every day until the wound had healed and meanwhile the hedgehog had to start a course of antibiotics. Only a veterinary surgeon can prescribe antibiotic drugs so Hannibal was the first of many hedgehogs seen on my behalf by Tuckett Gray and Partners at the Aylesbury Veterinary Hospital. A course of daily amoxycillin injections, given subcutaneously, was started – *and only someone who's been trained to give injections should attempt to inject animals* – using a 1 ml syringe marked in 1/10ths fitted with a 21 g × 16 mm (5/8 inch) needle, it's easier than it looks to pull up a bunch of spines just behind the hedgehog's neck and to slide the needle, at a very slight angle, just under the skin. Aspirating, that is pulling the plunger back, makes sure that no blood vessels have been entered before firmly administering the prescribed dose.

Needless to say, Hannibal did not relish this

Hannibal could peer down his nose at me.

treatment either and set off on one of his lopsided runs. I could envisage a troublesome week ahead but now that the course of antibiotics was started it had to be finished.

I had a collection of cages of all shapes and sizes so, as I wanted Hannibal to remain as clean as possible, I selected one with enough space to put his food well away from his bedding. Because of his open wound I decided not to give him hay but instead made a nest of newspaper torn into strips one inch wide. Any thinner and the strips might have tangled round a leg forming a tourniquet and causing him further problems. This is why the paper from a shredding machine is too fine to be used as nest material. A regular supply of hot water bottles made sure he did not go into hypothermic shock as a result of the anaesthetic.

It's strange how casualties always seem to turn up in twos or threes. The same evening as Hannibal arrived another hedgehog was brought in with a leg injury: she had black cotton wound around a front leg which once again protruded from an impregnable ball. She too did not like the ether pad but again I persevered and in no time had cut away the black ligature.

The skin had not been broken so a cage with a nice warm bed of hay, an anti-inflammatory beta-mesthasone injection given intra-muscularly by the vet and a few days' recuperation saw the swelling go down, the leg gradually disappear inside the impregnable ball and a hedgehog which was fit and nearly ready for release.

She appeared to be using her leg quite well; it was time to put her outside in one of the aviaries, in order to acclimatise her to the cool night air after the time spent in the warmed garage. A cosy nest box in the corner of the aviary where pigeons were convalescing before being released seemed ideal but I did not realise a hedgehog's hunting capability. On that first night outside, rather than eat her large bowl of Co-op Supermeat, she elected to grab one of the pigeons which had not made it to a high roost. Luckily I was outside and hearing the commotion managed to rescue Walter before any harm was done, except that the bird had shed handfuls of feathers. Walter soon settled down so I now had to find the disgruntled hedgehog fresh accommo-dation. I dared not put her in the corvid aviary – they would probably attack her as she would attack the kestrels if I put her with them – so I decided she would have to share with Chestnut, our lame squirrel. The arrangement worked well; after Chestnut's first investigation of his new room mate the only interest he showed was to raid her meat dish before she came out in the evening. Mind you, she also helped herself to his peanuts. Two weeks of this halcyon existence and she was ready to go but the question was where to release her?

Knowing that hedgehogs have a reasonable homing instinct I would have taken her to where she was originally found but there was the distinct possibility that she would end up tangled in more black cotton or would get run over on the busy main road which passed right in front of the house. It is estimated a hedgehog needs to forage over ten reasonable sized gardens, so I quizzed all our friends about theirs and their neighbours' gardens. I was looking in particular for a group of not very keen gardeners in whose gardens I could be sure there were no chemicals. Eventually I plumped for a 500 acre dairy farm where I could settle her into a nest box hoping she would not roam too far.

She stayed for a couple of nights and then disap-peared. Her natural instinct at work, I suppose, and although I worried about whether she had come to grief somewhere I had to let her take her chances as I would let any of our wild casualties. If I didn't, I would never release anything and would end up like some bird-of-prey rescue centres, a glorified menagerie.

Meanwhile, Hannibal's leg was responding to the daily cleaning and antibiotics: after only five days there was no more infected matter coming from the wound and it was starting to have a pink and healthy

Weighing in at St Tiggywinkles.

appearance. Over the next week the gaping hole seemed to heal from the inside. I stopped the antibiotics and four days later there was no sign of the abscess only a small area of pink bare skin showing where the wound had been.

He was still not using the leg which seemed stiff and slightly swollen but perhaps a few days' exercise would show an improvement. By now he was quite used to his daily manhandling and stopped curling up as I manipulated his leg joints. Laid on his back he would peer down his nose at me with a look of indignant resignation, not hesitating to squeal if I was a little too rough. I began to worry that the leg was not more flexible and about a swelling which had appeared on one side of his stomach just above the hip joint. Then, one day as I laid him down for his physiotherapy session, there was the matted underfur and tell-tale smell; all this time another abscess had been forming deep in his side.

I attempted to bathe the abscess but it must have been painful for Hannibal as he immediately curled up into a ball again. I could not take the chance of the infection spreading, so once again I resorted to the ether bottle and a fresh course of antibiotics. Being where it was, in the folds of his hip, it was very difficult to keep the abscess open and drained. It took two months to clear that abscess and a further three months before I was satisfied that he was not harbouring any other deep-seated infection.

Over the months I had grown to like old Hannibal and when the time came to release him it felt as though I was parting with a pet dog – but it had to be done. I need not have worried: Hannibal was released into the garden of good friends of ours who, although the hedgehog has no distinguishing marks, assure me that he still comes regularly for his dinner.

I insist on releasing any patient which is treated at St Tiggywinkles but always with the proviso that it is 100 per cent fit and fully capable of looking after itself in the wild. It's not easy being a wild animal eking an existence against fierce competition for food and living space: even the slightest impediment could mean a slow death by starvation or failure to react in time to avoid a predator or rival of the same species. Also to release an animal which suffers unnecessarily because it is not competent could be interpreted as abandonment as defined by the Protection of Animals Act 1911 and the Abandonment of Animals Act 1960, which of course only protect animals which are or have been in captivity.

Earthquake came to us in a very sorry state: he had been found floundering at the side of a busy road and had both eyes visibly destroyed as well as a broken bottom jaw that gaped loosely, permanently half open. A hedgehog does not rely on eyesight; its sense of smell and hearing are superbly designed to track down food in its nocturnal world. I could envisage a blind hedgehog living very comfortably in a totally enclosed, large garden where a regular nightly bowl of dog food would supplement the meagre diet to be found in one area only. Protection of this sort would be fine for the sightless hedgehog but he had the seemingly insurmountable problem of the broken jaw. Our vets, Russell Kilshaw and his colleagues, were getting used to me turning up with the most incredible demands on their expertise. They could wire together the broken symphysis in a hedgehog's jaw (where the two halves of the lower jaw meet at the front) but Earthquake's was broken at the back where the lower jaw hinges on the upper part of the skull. A fracture in this situation requires immobilisation with a stainless steel plate but hedgehogs are far too small to be operated on in this way and, needless to say, there are no stainless steel plates made small enough for the purpose. There was nothing which could be done. The hedgehog would probably die of starvation so I had seriously to contemplate asking the vets to destroy him humanely. But first we all agreed to wait 24 hours to see if we could come up with a solution.

The hedgehog had other ideas: I had put him in an intensive care cage and, without thinking, gave him bowls of food and water. I had turned away to contemplate his record card when the tell-tale slurp of a hedgehog relishing his food made me wonder if a strange hedgehog had been brought in without my knowledge. It was the injured animal: he was not going to let a simple thing like a broken jaw get in his way and he was demanding a second chance.

His stomach full of food, there was no way of holding him down; he turned his bowls upside down, tore the paper of his nest into shreds and mixed the resulting mixture of paper, dog food and water with the towel we used to line his cage. Over and over he turned the mess and added some of his own to the gooey upheaval.

I changed everything, wiped him off and put him back in his cage. No sooner had I closed the door than off he went again, more paper, hedgehog droppings, dog food and water: Earthquake was the obvious name for him.

After four weeks he was as destructive as ever but was still eating most of his food; any leftovers were promptly mixed with his bedding and water dish. His jaw was working well although he could not quite close his mouth, but that did not seem to bother him. He was ready to go outside into one of the larger pens where he could 'earthquake' as much as he wanted without having to be cleaned out four or five times a day.

I had recently built a plastic pen with rigid mesh supplied by Netlon which he could bump into without damaging his frail snout or already injured eyes. We put him directly into a brand new nest box, full of sweet fresh hay and some of his old bedding so that he would know where to go for shelter. He liked that, 'earthquaked' it and then set about exploring the new scents in the rest of the pen. On his first circuit he collided with everything but on the second lap he knew where the obstacles were and avoided them without hesitating. He soon found his food, had a good meal and a drink of water and then returned to his box, 'earthquaked' it again and settled down for a rest.

From then on he acted just like a normal hedgehog, except that, not being able to tell light from dark, he would quite often appear during the day to investigate new scents and snap up unwary insects. He even worked out his own jogging track in a figure of eight around an old stump, across and round the trunk of a willow then back across and round the stump again. He would follow this exact route, sometimes for half an hour or more then, all of a sudden, for no apparent reason, he would stop, turn and head straight back to his nest box, which, needless to say, was 'earthquaked' again. There has always been a mystery as to why some solitary hedgehogs are seen running in circles. Every blind hedgehog we have had since Earthquake has done this so it's possible that any hedgehog behaving in this way may have eye problems of some kind. The circling of a courting male hedgehog around a female is quite different as there is always more than one participant and the circle is usually much smaller.

Hedgehogs are typically solitary animals. Earthquake had lived alone for some months when we found that we needed to put a recovered female patient out into a safe pen while she became used

Love that brings hope to the wild

Report :
EMMA LEE-POTTER
Pictures :
MIKE LAWN

LES STOCKER had no idea what he was letting himself in for when he rescued a squirrel that had been run over.

After he and his wife, Sue, took it to the local vet, they were appalled to discover later it had been put down.

"We felt we had murdered him," said Sue, 40.

It was from this one incident that the Wildlife Hospital Trust was born.

Run by the Stockers from their small back garden on a residential estate in Aylesbury, Bucks, it rescues wild animals, cares for them and then returns them to the wild.

"We felt terrible because we thought his injuries possibly did not warrant him being put down," said Les, 42, a former accountant who now works as a freelance writer.

How many other wild animals were suffering, they wondered, simply because there were too few people who knew how to treat them.

In 1977 the couple threw caution to the winds and set up their own small wildlife

FIRST AID : two Little Owls, bandaged after being hit by cars.

hospital, helped by a local vet. They believe it is the only one of its kind in the country.

The Stockers' garden is now full of rows of small cages, all built by Les.

A fox found on a railway line suffering from a cerebral haemorrhage sunbathes on top of its box while Betty, an adult badger, the Stockers believe was the victim of badger baiting, is curled up under a mass of straw.

"I cannot believe what some people do to animals," said Sue angrily. "It is quite beyond my imagination how someone can get joy out of harming them."

Volunteers

At the moment they are looking after about 170 animals, ranging from newborn hedgehogs to an injured swan.

Two years ago the Stockers decided to set up the trust, a registered charity, to cope with the cost of caring for the animals. Just looking after one baby hedgehog — they have more than 70 at the moment— costs £3·50 a week, while a swan costs them £24.

A devoted team of volunteers, many of them schoolchildren, come in each day to help with the work.

Meanwhile, the trust has gone from strength to strength. It has 700 members and publishes its own magazine called Bright Eyes twice a year. Last year a total of 4000 animals passed through the Stockers' caring hands which is why the trust is now involved in fund-raising to build a new wildlife hospital.

As for the Stockers, the hospital has simply taken over their lives. The telephone rings at all hours as people from all over the country report injured animals they have found, or ask about creatures they have bought in.

"We never go out and we haven't had a holiday for eight years," said Sue. "We keep saying we'll go away next week but we would worry terribly. We would want to know what was going on."

● Chessington Zoo's polar bears Bonnie and Clyde are to get a larger bear pit, ready for when they start breeding.

The zoo is spending £100,000 on extension work this winter, during which Bonnie and Clyde will have to move to another zoo.

to the cooler nights outside. There was plenty of space in Earthquake's aviary so we put in another nest box and introduced the female, but watched very carefully in case either hedgehog behaved aggressively.

Quite the contrary: on that first night when the female ventured out of her box Earthquake immediately scented her presence, abandoned his jogging track and made towards her puffing like an old steam engine. Would he attempt to 'earthquake' this interloper? No, Earthquake showed for the first time that he had a refined side to his nature and began circling the lady in good hedgehog tradition but instead of making the headlong dash of the less debonair male, he swaggered around her at a snail's pace, swaying his hips like some prickly flamenco dancer. The lady was not impressed and constantly butted her suitor off his stride. Not to be deterred, Earthquake serenaded his lady every night but to no avail. Even when we introduced a second female he spent his nights fruitlessly alternating between one and the other.

Before long both his lady-loves were fit and were released but Earthquake did not have to spend much time on his own, for shortly afterwards a blind female was brought in to St Tiggywinkles. She had been kicked by some boys and as well as being blinded she was in a severe state of shock and concussion. Given subcutaneous fluids to counteract the dehydration caused by shock she was kept warm on a constant supply of hot water bottles covered with old towels to prevent her being scalded. We were greatly concerned that her brain might have been damaged by the incident. There is no recovery from that, but happily after two days of warmth and quiet she made her first efforts to walk and on the third day managed to drink some of the electrolyte replacement, Lectade, we had offered in the place of water.

Electrolytes are chemicals like sodium, potassium and chloride, necessary for some of the metabolic processes of the body. Any imbalance of these, especially through shock and dehydration, can seriously endanger the life of an animal and they need to be replaced before any other rehydration can take effect.

By the second week of confinement, the concussed hedgehog was behaving normally, that is for a blind hedgehog, so we installed her in the spare box in Earthquake's pen. They hit it off straight away and contrary to hedgehog practice spent all their sleeping hours curled up together in his box. His swaggering paid off and Mrs Earthquake gave birth to two minute little pin-cushions. We did have to split them up while the babies grew just in case he mistook them for a tasty meal. They have now been released but Earthquake and his lady still live happily in the plastic pen until the perfect walled garden is offered as a home for them.

For those readers who, though they would like to help an injured animal, may be finding some of the veterinary and occasionally gory detail in this chapter a bit beyond their capabilities, and even perhaps upsetting, here is a check list of basic **First Aid measures** which should be applied if you find an injured hedgehog, and which may help to save it even before you manage to take it to the vet:

1. Keep the animal warm with direct **heat, either with a hot water bottle (wrapped in a towel) or with an overhead heat source.**
2. Offer it water with a little glucose dissolved in it – never **milk or alcohol.**

3. Dust any maggots with Negasunt (don't worry about fleas or ticks) and bathe any wounds with warm, dilute **Savlon.**

4. Burns should be covered with a cold towel or a cold compress, never apply any type of grease or ointment.

5. Oil can be removed with Co-op washing-up liquid (see below). Tar can be loosened with Swarfega (see p.123).

6. Take it to the vet or to St Tiggywinkles.

And here is a list of standard hedgehog **First Aid kit** to keep handy for these emergencies:

Savlon	cottonwool
Co-op washing-up	
liquid	**cotton buds**
tweezers	**plastic bowl**
rubber gloves	**Swarfega**
clean old towels	**hot water bottle**
newspapers	**a good cardboard box**
scissors	**a tub of Negasunt**
a tin of Pedigree	**Rid-Mite flea**
Chum Puppy	**powder**
Food	**(pyrethrum)**

In the following pages are some more precise descriptions, based on actual incidents, of these basic techniques and First Aid measures as well as more complicated procedures some of which could be undertaken by those who regularly look after injured animals. **In the serious cases, as most of the drugs and remedies must be administered under the auspices of a sympathetic vet, kitchen sink remedies are not enough.**

Eyes   Some hedgehogs may be found running in circles and appear to be blind with their eyelids firmly shut. Bathing the eyes with warmed water should enable you to check inside the eye to see if there is damage or more importantly if any maggots have made their way in. Any maggots should be picked out with blunt forceps or tweezers and any damage left alone as the eye has remarkable powers of self recovery. Sometimes getting the vet to suture the eyelids together will help an eye heal, especially if there is a loss of eye fluids. Any signs of pus or other infection should be washed out with saline solution or warm water but if the conjunctivitis persists then a course of chloramphenicol eye ointment can be obtained from the vet if he examines the hedgehog first.

Ears   While checking the eyes it's always worthwhile inspecting the ears for maggots (which can be flushed out with warmed dilute Savlon) or the waxy build up that can be a sign of mite infestation. Once again your vet should be able to supply cerumen penetrating and softening drops which will not only ease the hedgehog's discomfort but may help destroy any parasites, bacteria or fungus. The resulting goo can be gently swabbed out with small cotton buds.

Oil   As we see more and more hedgehogs we are constantly amazed at the predicaments into which they get themselves. Much of our treatment has to be based on improvisation because as yet there is often no recognised standard practice. Take, for example, the many hedgehogs which seem to find their way into trays or even open tins of oil. If they were birds, there would be a standard practice to deal with them, using methods devised by the University of Newcastle-upon-Tyne. When the first oiled hedgehogs came in we gave them the same treatment: a 2 per cent solution of Co-op washing-up liquid (it must be Co-op, no other brand works so well) was made up in a bowl at 45°C. The little hedgehog, Castro, was almost totally immersed for ten seconds. He opened up automatically and then the hand hot solution was worked into his spines and underbody fur. He did not like the manhandling but I am sure his struggles helped to loosen the stubborn oil. His head was lightly scrubbed with an old toothbrush dipped in the solution until the water looked black and he looked more like a hedgehog. We rinsed him thoroughly, again at 45°C, using a hose shower attachment fitted on our bath taps. Unlike birds which should be allowed to drip dry, Castro was rubbed nearly dry with a warm fluffy towel and put under a heat lamp to dry off

Sometimes new inmates will be attacked by resident patients.

completely. He had not suffered from either of his ordeals and was soon tucking into a bowl of dog food. We checked his faeces for some days but he did not seem to have swallowed any of the oil which could seriously have damaged his stomach lining. If there had been traces of oil from his stomach, we would have put him on the same treatment prescribed for birds in a similar condition – a course of kaolin-based sulphadimidine containing some antibiotic, usually neomycin.

Tar   Tar Baby, as his name suggests, had gone one better than Castro and had managed to walk into a heap of wet tar which was still clinging to his feet when he was brought into St Tiggywinkles. We tried the Co-op washing-up liquid treatment to no avail; lighter fuel and paraffin had no effect; we even tried butter and margarine. Things were looking desperate as the tar was likely to harden at any time, when I had a brainwave: we all use Swarfega to remove oil, grease or paint from our hands, so why not try it on this tiny hedgehog? It worked like a dream, softening the tar so that we could wipe the feet clean, finally rinsing them off with warm soapy water. Luckily he had not burned his skin with the hot tar but I applied some petroleum jelly just to ease the stiffness.

Burns   Burnt hedgehogs are often brought in to us, especially in the autumn when heaps of leaves and Guy Fawkes' bonfires are set alight without being checked for hedgehog occupants. Superficial burns where the skin is reddened and the spines singed should be cleaned with dilute Savlon to prevent contamination. The spines, which are after all only modified hairs, can be clipped short with a sharp pair of nail scissors. If the hedgehog is found within ten minutes of being burned, apply a cold towel that has been soaked in cold water, and wrung out, to the burns for ten minutes to help dissipate the heat. Dry the area with sterile gauze swabs but do not apply any medication and *definitely no oil, grease or butter* which only serve to trap the heat in the wound.

Deeper burns, second or third degree, where the skin and underlying tissues are severely damaged should be referred to a veterinary surgeon. You can help initially with first aid by applying sterile localised cold compresses to the wounds and covering them with clean towels to prevent contamination. The hedgehog will probably be in deep shock and must be kept warm. Subcutaneous fluids and an electrolyte replacer taken orally will help an animal during the initial aftermath before the vet can see it.

Chemical burns from tins and batteries left lying in garages are all too common with hedgehogs. It is absolutely essential to flush the hedgehog's skin for five minutes using a shower attachment and cool water. If you can find the container the chemical was in it should state whether it is acid or alkali. After the initial five-minute flushing with cool water an equal part of water and vinegar can be used to sponge alkali burns, while three tablespoons of baking soda in 2¼ litres of warm water should be sponged onto acid burns. After flushing and sponging, cover the areas with sterile gauze dressings and offer electrolyte replacer to counteract shock.

With all burns where the outer skin layer is damaged there is nothing to stop infection so a course of antibiotics is called for, but *burns can produce so many complications that it is imperative to consult a veterinary surgeon.*

'Balloon' syndrome (subcutaneous emphysema)   Some hedgehog casualties have baffled us even when we have managed to treat them. Twice now we have had hedgehogs brought in which were blown up like balloons with their skin as tight as drums. We could not trace what had caused this subcutaneous emphysema: it might have been a gas-gangrene caused by an old wound. With a sterile needle and a syringe with a small tap fitted to it we managed to draw the gas off until the hedgehog was its normal size again, although its stretched skin hung around its body like curtains. A course of antibiotics was necessary to control the infection which had caused the 'blow-up' but as yet we have not traced the source.

Nose injury   The most peculiar injury that is commonly brought to us is a hedgehog with the end of its nose, the rhinarium, sliced through. One case looked as though the hedgehog had walked onto a circular saw which had sliced its nose completely in half. One side was hanging down uselessly so Russell, our vet, removed this with thermo-cautery. After a course of antibiotics and regular bathing of the area all the nose jobs have been released functioning, that is dripping, as a healthy hedgehog's nose should.

The hedgehog on the right is suffering from the strange but easily remedied 'balloon' syndrome.

Fractures and Paralysis Where there has been no specific injury but obvious lameness we have had to assume that there has been nerve or muscle damage. Twisted necks, hanging limbs and failure to roll up are all typical symptoms where it is a case of wait and see. Fortunately in most cases improvement has been noticed after a couple of weeks. Sometimes the hedgehog is temporarily incapable of reaching into a food dish and needs to be held up in order to feed or drink. Although it makes a mess of the pen it often helps to put dog food directly on to the floor of the pen: we often have hedgehogs lying on their sides scoffing away in true hedgehog fashion. We have recently had a patient, Ernie, who could not stand up following a hernia operation. He fed well from the floor and only had to be lifted up to his water bowl to drink.

Flaccid paralysis of both back legs may be due to nerve or muscle damage but an X-ray is vital in case there is a fractured pelvis or damage to the spine. If there is no obvious injury, a deficiency of some of the B vitamins could be the cause – curable by a simple course of the missing vitamins. Oral administration with Abidec baby vitamins, SA 37 or Vet-amin is the most effective method but, if the hedgehog is not co-operative, an injection may be called for.

I transport all suspected fracture cases to the veterinary hospital in a solid plastic box allowing the hedgehog as little space as possible in order not to aggravate the injury. Hedgehogs are notorious for walking on fractured limbs causing the sharp broken ends of the bone to pierce the skin, risking infection and seriously hampering the healing process. Strapping the fractured limb or limbs to simple splints will prevent any unnecessary complications before a vet can be consulted. An ice-lolly stick or even a piece of broken pencil will do as a splint but do not wrap the limb too securely – remember the vet has to remove all the adhesive tape before he or she can work on the injury. A single piece of tape securing each side of the fracture can be simply cut away without putting any stress on the injury or the vet.

Dehydration: Warmth and Fluids It's October while I write this and judging by last year's experience and the present influx of casualties, hedgehogs do not, as has been suggested, think of hibernation so early. They prefer to wait until late November before settling down for their winter sleep. At this time of year we receive hedgehogs of all shapes and sizes, from 90 gram babies without their eyes open to 1200 gram casualties, but by far the most common patients are the juveniles, weighing about 230 grams, which have been found lying out in the open during the day. Any hedgehog whether young or old found out during the day is in trouble and needs attention before the local blow flies and magpies can take advantage of its vulnerability. These juveniles are no exception, but it's still a mystery whether it is the transition from their mothers' feeding to a completely wild existence or their first intake of cow's milk which causes nearly all these youngsters to have stomach upsets, producing liquid faeces, and the consequent dehydration and debility.

Of course a faeces sample analysis would give a more specific answer but invariably these hedgehogs are near to death and need immediate medical attention. The symptoms become all too familiar: a semi-comatose hedgehog which shows no inclination to curl up; the bright button eyes are partially closed; the skin which should feel taut hangs down around its sides like a deflated paper bag: the stomach which should be full and round is empty; and the hedgehog is cold to touch.

Two things will keep the young hedgehog alive in this condition: warmth and fluids. If no sophisticated form of direct heat is available, place the hedgehog on a hot water bottle wrapped in an old towel. Radiators are just not good enough and trying to treat a casualty in an outside shed or garage can only end in failure. Ignore any fleas and bring the casualty into the house in a deep-sided cardboard box.

Administering subcutaneous fluids is the other life-saving procedure which should be considered for a wildlife casualty appearing listless, dull eyed and dehydrated – quite a simple procedure for a vet or if your vet shows you what to do. To administer subcutaneous fluids, take a 10 ml syringe fitted with a 21 g × 16 mm (5/8 inch) needle and, using one of the hedgehog's spines, pull up a fold of skin well forward on its back to either side of the centre, being careful to avoid the spinal column, and slide the needle into the skin more or less parallel to the surface. Pull the plunger back slightly to make sure you have not punctured a blood vessel then slowly inject 5 per cent of the hedgehog's bodyweight of physiological saline, a sterile mixture of dextrose and sodium chloride prescribable only by a veterinary surgeon. A hedgehog weighing 500 grams would receive 25 ml of fluid but care must be taken not to try to squeeze it all into one site; two or three different entry points on opposite sides of the back will cause less distress to the hedgehog. At the same time a subcutaneous injection of vitamin B complex diluted with dextrose saline solution will help balance any vitamin deficiencies and may well help any hedgehog which has eaten poison.

If you regularly look after sick and injured animals then, rather than relying on hot water bottles, it's worth investing in some form of overhead heating lamp. Mammals are generally blind to red light so a red coloured or photographic bulb suspended just above the casualty will have the desired warming effect without startling the animal. We are only trying to maintain body heat so make sure the animal doesn't overheat and at all times can escape to a cooler part of its pen if it wishes. More sophisticated and economical, although initially more expensive, are the ceramic heat lamps which show no light and where all the energy is converted directly into heat. More powerful than the simple red bulb they have to be suspended higher over the patient. The Salamander range manufactured by Infrared International in Cork in Ireland are made in various wattages but the smallest at 100 watts should cope with any hedgehog's heating problems. Adult hedgehogs should be kept at about 25°C with youngsters somewhat warmer, up to 35°C for newborn babies.

Once the hedgehog is warmer it will start to move and look much brighter, and now is the time to administer a minute dose of wormer onto its tongue. It should swallow automatically and may now even lap up water if this is offered in a shallow dish. Check the hedgehog's bottom, or its faeces if it has passed any, looking for traces of diarrhoea and blood which may signify the presence of coccidia in its intestines. Coccidia will respond only to treatment by one of the sulphonamides. If you suspect coccidia – and analysis of a stool sample will confirm whether or not they are present – routinely dose the hedgehog with a sulphadimidine–kaolin mixture for five days.

It's usual to starve an animal with an enteric disorder for 24 hours but these juvenile hedgehogs are usually weak, having not eaten for some days. Often a low dish of cooked chicken or something light will entice the hedgehog into activity, but *on no account should bread or milk be offered* because it acts as a breeding ground for the bacteria we are trying to destroy. In its place, and in place of water, an electrolyte replacing fluid should be offered to help reverse the dehydration. However, if after eight hours the hedgehog is still not looking brighter, administer another subcutaneous injection of dextrose saline solution, this time about half the quantity.

Resuscitation   Invariably some hedgehogs are so debilitated as to be beyond the point of no return and no matter what measures you take to save them, they will sadly die. It's going to happen, so be prepared for it, but before you finally give up on a casualty make sure that rigor mortis has set in. Whenever one of my hedgehogs dies I take it as a failure and dispose of the body as quickly as possible, but I learned my lesson in the early days when one poor creature which I was about to bury moved a leg. I hurriedly gave it subcutaneous fluids and warmth and saw it revive and grow into a very fit and healthy hedgehog which gave me pangs of guilt every time I looked at it. From then on I always leave a potential corpse until rigor mortis is obvious and I have invested in a stethoscope in order to trace any flicker of a heartbeat.

If there is a heartbeat but no sign of breathing, simple artificial respiration of the chest may well restore it, but *on no account should mouth to mouth resuscitation be contemplated,* just in case the animal is suffering from a disease contagious to man. After all, who would replace you in caring for hedgehogs if you were no longer around?

Open Wounds   Any hedgehog with an open wound should be kept completely separate from other hedgehogs as they might consider attacking and damaging the injured areas. One particular hedgehog which is still with us carried the habit one degree further and started biting his own wounds. We had a call from Cheltenham that a large hedgehog had been found in serious difficulties. As luck would have it two of our regular helpers, Jan and Jeff Loveridge, were due back from Wales the following day, would be passing Cheltenham and could pick up Elvis, as he came to be known, on their way through.

Elvis: Multiple Injuries and a Broken Pelvis   When Elvis

Often young hedgehogs put their heads through rings or sections of pipe left lying around, and then grow into them – sometimes with tragic results.

arrived we found that he had suffered appalling injuries, probably the result of collision with a motor car. His back right leg was so badly broken and infected that Russell had no alternative but to amputate. The other back leg was also badly infected but not broken so there was hope that it would heal. To cap it all he also had a broken pelvis. In spite of all this, there was a strong possibility that he would heal although there was no way of fixing the broken pelvis since, as with Earthquake's jaw, there was nothing small enough to do the job. However, with a period of close confinement it was possible that it would heal spontaneously within four to five weeks.

After the first day in confinement Elvis displayed the classic signs often resulting from a broken pelvis: he could not urinate. He had to be helped otherwise the build up of unevacuated toxins in his body could prove disastrous. With larger animals like cats and dogs it is possible to slide a catheter up the urinary tract into the bladder allowing it to drain by pressure but, as always, hedgehogs are too small for this method of treatment. Every day, until it recovered and worked normally, I would have to locate his bladder – like a small hard balloon in the abdomen – and squeeze it very gently, expelling any urine that had collected. This has to be done very carefully because the membrane forming the skin of the bladder is so fine, and often so stretched, that there is a risk of rupturing the bladder, causing uraemia and peritonitis, which would be fatal. Elvis, however, was large and robust and so far I have managed to avoid that kind of accident.

Then, as if he didn't have enough problems, Elvis decided to try to eat the foot on his remaining back leg. Even without the other back leg his future was doubtful; without either of them there was no future whatsoever. However, there was always a chance that the torn leg and foot would regenerate, as long as I prevented Elvis from attacking it. Dogs and cats can be fitted with large plastic collars to prevent them aggravating a wound but – you've guessed it – a hedgehog is too small for one of those and too large for those designed for pet mice and guinea pigs. The damaged foot would have to be bandaged although I knew that being enclosed the wounds would take much longer to heal. Bathing with Dermisol would help, and a non-stick dressing pad held in place by a bandage and adhesive tape should protect the wound from Elvis. This dressing would have to be changed every day but as his pelvis prevented him from rolling up it was not too difficult to get at.

Every night now for almost a month I have cleaned and redressed that foot and precariously emptied his bladder and still he makes no attempt to use his pelvis or pass water on his own. I think I know, deep down, that there is no hope but I have made the terrible mistake of getting too close to Elvis and his bright-eyed spirit and am now finding it difficult to face the inevitable. Perhaps I will give him another week or two before I get somebody else to take him to the vet.

Mucking out   In many ways Elvis is just like any other hedgehog casualty: he eats well, relishing his food, greeting us every morning with it daubed all round his pen; no sooner have you replaced his bedding than he finds a way to mess it up. Elvis, in necessary confinement, is in a cage measuring 40 centimetres by 30 centimetres whereas other casualties have twice that amount of space, which means double the amount to be cleaned out every morning. Food and water dishes serve as toilets and any dressings are used to wipe or stir all manner of messy concoctions. These all have to be cleaned or changed every day. Caring for hedgehogs is not for those who like to keep their hands clean. Fortunately, some cases need be kept in intensive care only overnight – the sooner a wildlife casualty is outside the better it seems to be.

'Pop-off' syndrome   One condition which requires only an overnight stay is a problem that could only occur in hedgehogs. It's never been recorded in the medical journals so we call it 'pop-off syndrome', which aptly describes how the dorsal spiny skin is somehow pushed up over the hedgehog's haunches with the orbicularis muscle springing tight and preventing the skin from returning to its normal position. When it happens the hedgehog's legs are forced sideways, the anal orifice and tail are pulled up over the back and the hedgehog is completely helpless. The condition is probably caused by some form of traumatic accident: the only case I ever saw, *in situ* so to speak, was a female which had got herself firmly wedged between some wire netting and a wooden fence. In her struggles to escape the orbicularis muscle had slipped over her haunches, right up over her back.

Once the skin has 'popped off' it is a physical impossibility to pull the muscles back to their normal position. However, anaesthetising the animal, thus relaxing the muscles, allows the hedgehog to be pulled into its normal shape. The condition does not seem to recur spontaneously, so after a short period of observation the animal may be released, which is particularly important if a female casualty may have dependent youngsters waiting for her.

Before embarking on treatment for 'pop-off syndrome', note whether the back legs, which are invariably set askew, are rigid or flaccid. Pinch the toes with a pair of forceps to see if the hedgehog flinches. If it registers no reaction, then make no attempt to manipulate the hedgehog but very carefully arrange to have it X-rayed as there is a possibility that it has damaged the vertebral column.

As I have said and proved, on hundreds of occasions, hedgehogs are perfectly capable of recovering from the most horrendous injuries provided that the highest quality medical care and nursing is offered to them. Isolate all new cases, keep them warm and clean, follow the veterinarian's instructions to the letter and always complete a course of antibiotics. Only use syringes and needles once, then dispose of them *safely* and boil all medical instruments each time you use them. Take note of your hedgehog's general demeanour and whether it regularly passes faeces and urine. Keeping casualties in separate cages will make it easier to spot problems: a hedgehog which does not eat its food could be in difficulties and need extra attention.

Hopefully, any hedgehogs will recover from their ailments and can be considered for release. As I have said, they need at least ten reasonable sized gardens in which to find enough food to survive, and should not be released near to a fast or fairly busy road. One point to remember when releasing a hedgehog is not to be swayed by stories like 'there are no hedgehogs in this area – we'd like to re-introduce them'. I know the idea of filling nature's vacuum is appealing but there may be good reason why there are no hedgehogs in an area: it may be too draughty, there may be pollution or no natural food, there may be badgers in the vicinity, it may be too dry. Only hedgehogs know why they have avoided one area, so take notice of their absence and release your animals in a hedgehog populated area. We always release our hedgehogs via a nest box so that they have somewhere to go if nest sites are hard to find.

Sometimes we are so busy that we have to keep more than one hedgehog to a pen which can make identification of individuals difficult. Rather than paint numbers or spots on them or cut patterns out of their spines, we use multi-coloured bugle beads, one of which can be slid onto a single spine and held in place by a minute dab of glue. Individual colours can then identify individual hedgehogs and when the hedgehog is released the marked spine can simply be trimmed back with a pair of sharp scissors.

Much of this chapter has been about the type of first aid which most people, with a little consideration and some skill, can practise to help hedgehogs, but *always remember that if your hedgehog casualty is severely injured or is not responding to treatment, you should refer it to a sympathetic veterinary surgeon.*

Andrew Hawley

Operation Hedgehog

IT'S THE fear that an animal may be severely injured which makes us encourage people to phone us at any time of the day or night if they have found a casualty. In fact we try to sound cheerful, even if we have woken from a deep sleep. Nonetheless, it's always ominous when you receive a call after midnight as it usually means that there is a badger or deer or fox lying by the road somewhere. Hedgehogs never seem to be found after about 11 o'clock, just as public houses are closing. Patches was the exception: a frantic phone call at two o'clock in the morning from a doctor in Berkhamsted soon brought the hedgehog, nearly comatose, to our door.

As with most of our patients, we shall never know what happened to him. His skin had been almost completely ripped off, exposing, under their thin layer of membrane, the major panniculus and orbicularis muscles. Only his legs held the remaining skin to his body: it seemed as though he could literally have stepped out of his skin.

He obviously needed urgent medical treatment to counteract the severe shock which had made him completely unconscious. Our surgery was across the garden and as it was now two-thirty Sue and I tiptoed out so as not to disturb not only the other patients but also our neighbours. Very carefully I prepared the surgery without even the customary 'clunks' as I loaded the steriliser with any instruments I might need to clean up the wounds.

Turning my attention to Patches who was lying on the heat pad, I saw no signs of any drastic blood loss. He needed fluid therapy to counteract his obvious dehydration but he had no skin under which to put my subcutaneous injections of dextrose saline. Very carefully I managed to insert 50 mls under the membrane which covered the muscles. He made no movement or sign of protest, from which I could deduce that he was unaware of any pain sensation. Quickly checking the amount of skin still attached along his sides I estimated that it would be possible completely to cover his back but that the treatment had to be started immediately before the natural healing processes sealed the exposed edges.

There was bound to be some infection because of the amount of grit and dirt adhering to the exposed surfaces. For an hour I carefully swabbed off, with warmed dilute Savlon, any contamination I could find. He still made no movement of protest and it was his severe state of shock which worried me.

It was now three-thirty. He was so oblivious to

Patches soon made a remarkable recovery.

sensation that I decided to go ahead and attempt suturing without any further delay. Russell always says that where there is some bleeding on the edge of skin wounds there is a greater likelihood of a good healing union. As I pulled the first two pieces of skin together I could see how pink the edges were. I was suturing just in time. Patches obviously did not feel a thing. If there had been any pain, he would have needed anaesthetising which in view of his depressed condition could have been a problem. As it was, after half an hour's painstaking needlework he looked like a hedgehog again, even though I had found it necessary to clip away many of his spines.

We had been very quiet all through the procedure until just as I was bathing his freshly sutured wounds the peace of the night was shattered by the harsh clanging of an alarm bell. I fell out of the surgery to see what it was. A flashing orange light bombarded around the garden, the kestrels started screaming and the stone curlew was frantic in its effort to escape the mayhem.

Our new neighbours, it seemed, had outdone the Joneses by having a burglar alarm fitted to the back of their house. One by one every household around was wakened; all the lights went on and bleary-eyed sleepers peered out of their windows at the light show. So much for our small attempts not to wake the neighbours!

They managed to stop the clanging as Patches, feeling the benefit of the warmth and fluids, started to revive. He moved around, rather stiffly but at least he no longer looked like something out of a biology lesson at school.

We expected some infection in spite of the course of antibiotics but even the small patch behind his left ear responded to Dermisol. After six weeks only the track of the clipped spines showed the extent of the scarring. Patches was to all intents and purposes a normal hedgehog again except, that is, in one department: he had lost so much skin that until he regained his elasticity he just could not roll up. Added to this he showed himself to be a hearty feeder and was in danger of becoming hopelessly overweight.

Over the weeks he had been, by necessity, handled a great deal and seemed unbothered by people so when we were asked by the BBC to take a hedgehog onto *Pebble Mill at One*, Patches was the automatic choice, along with Earthquake, another of our long-term inmates.

At Pebble Mill, Patches met Wendy Richard of the *EastEnders* TV series. He now looked most handsome even though he was fairly corpulent by this time. Wendy fell for him and promptly joined St Tiggywinkles Adoption Scheme to sponsor his upkeep.

The great moment arrived, the arc lights were on, the cameras rolling, Earthquake was doing his best to destroy his bedding but, as Bob Langley started the interview, Patches, whom I was holding, refused to move. I am sure that whoever saw him on television that day imagined he was stuffed. We resolved to put him on a diet and into a larger pen where he would get more exercise.

At the time a female hedgehog and her well grown babies occupied an aviary to themselves so it was with her that I put Patches. All was fine until Patches decided to court the female in the age old hedgehog tradition. But as he circled her and she responded with head butts he could not roll up to protect his flanks so he was thrown onto his back, kicking in the air and unable to regain an upright position. It seemed that Patches, for the moment, would have to live on his own.

Patches settled into a cosy enclosed pen lined with

fresh hay. At least I would now be able to control his diet. The weight-watching worked and Patches slimmed down to become a very active hedgehog – but he still could not roll up.

All went well until the winter. After the first frost, on my usual morning rounds, I looked in and found Patches. My heart sank. He looked dead. I carried him inside to tell Sue but as I went through the kitchen I noticed a slight movement in one of his front legs. Gently I warmed him. He was not dead after all but being unable to roll up he had hibernated as stiff as a board. In this prostrate position he had no protection from the cold so I had to move him inside with all the winter orphans which were too small to hibernate. He now shares a large heated cage with another adult male hedgehog which is fortunately not aggressive towards his plump friend. Patches still tries to eat too much but looks as handsome as ever, even after all his ordeals.

In the case of Patches I did not need to call Russell out for the initial treatment even though I asked him to check the patient the following day. I try to respect a vet's time off and will only bother him after his normal surgery hours in emergencies or when I have a rush of casualties needing urgent attention. He is always more than willing to drop whatever he is doing in order to help an animal in distress.

Bank holidays are always a busy time for us: people are out and about gardening, walking, driving, jogging, cycling and consequently finding wildlife casualties which are probably missed on normal working days. On an August Bank Holiday Monday the surgery at Tuckett Gray and Partners, our vets, looked like a hedgehog disaster area. The surgery was closed for normal business but so great was the weekend's influx of hedgehog casualties to St

A hedgehog anaesthetic apparatus – the best way to unroll a stubborn casualty.

Tiggywinkles that Russell had suggested I take them all down there while the surgery was empty.

In amongst the steam from the steriliser and Russell's hurried lunch were box after box of impregnable balls of hedgehog with legs sticking out in all

For a longer operation the hedgehog has to be put into a face mask fitted to full anaesthetic equipment.

directions. My initial diagnoses back at the hospital had indicated several fractures. We knew, therefore, that many would have to be X-rayed.

X-raying impregnable balls would be pointless so each hedgehog needs to be anaesthetised for a preliminary assessment of its injuries. There are many ways of anaesthetising hedgehogs but some recommended methods need an unrolled hedgehog, something we did not have.

When Russell first started working on my hedgehog casualties he would unroll them with a subcutaneous injection of ketamine hydrochloride followed, for a long anaestheic, by halothane and oxygen administered through a small face mask. Lengthier anaesthesia with analgesia could have been arranged using ketamine and xylazine but, because of the difficulty of intramuscular injection, its results are unpredictable. When one is dealing with large numbers of patients, costs have to be considered, especially when there is an alternative that is both cheap and controllable, with good analgesic and recovery properties.

We have found that a simple anaesthetic chamber fed with halothane and oxygen produces good anaesthesia and has reliable recovery properties. Once the patient is unrolled, a small face mask on a standard Fluotec machine gives perfect control over the animal's consciousness. Although it is impossible to use endotracheal tubes with hedgehogs, they never seem to require the length of anaesthesia which might produce a respiratory emergency. They remain reasonably stable under halothane, unlike many other types of wildlife, especially deer, which need constant monitoring and adjusting.

The first hedgehog in the chamber had been brought down from Nottingham. I suspected a fracture of the femur but there was doubt about its pelvis as well. Lying it on its back in the chamber with its obviously damaged leg poking from its centre allowed us to judge the moment it relaxed and could be unrolled. A hedgehog's legs are surprisingly long and can be extended over the X-ray plate to give a good radiograph.

The X-ray confirmed that it had fractured its femur but that the pelvis looked unscathed. Usually with the femur of a small animal an intramedullary pin would be the only way of obtaining a good enough fixation for the bone to heal but as a pin would have to be brought out through the hip the amount of muscle and other tissue in a hedgehog's hindquarters made this method difficult without causing damage and possible complications. In larger animals stainless steel plates can be fitted onto the femur itself, but as usual with hedgehogs, there is nothing made small enough – although I have just obtained some tiny finger plates which I might persuade Russell to try on the next fractured femur. As it was, we decided to restrict severely the movement of this hedgehog. There was a good chance that the fracture would mend spontaneously in a reasonable position.

The next hedgehog, Hissing Sid, bucked and hissed as I picked him out of his box but two minutes in the chamber saw him sleeping like a baby. He did not need an X-ray as he obviously had a simple fracture of the tibia which had pierced the skin. Although the wound was reasonably fresh there was no doubt that there would have been some infection already. The fracture reduced very well so after cleaning the wound Russell covered it with a non-adherent perforated film absorbent dressing and fitted a standard plaster-of-Paris cast. Because of the infection this would have to be changed regularly – at which times it is worth monitoring the inevitable pressure sores which appear above the plaster. A course of lincomycin injection helped control the infection.

This must have been the umpteenth plaster cast Russell had fitted to a hedgehog so we were all a bit surprised when a television news item showed another veterinary surgeon claiming a first in treating a hedgehog's fractured leg. In fact one tiny young hedgehog which had arrived in the spring, soon after hibernation, had two plaster casts fitted by Russell, one to its front left leg and the other to its hind left leg. I am sure that the plaster casts were heavier than the hedgehog itself but it managed to get around, even though I had to help it up to food and water bowls. The animal was so small that it was a miracle that it survived hibernation and even more amazing that it could have lived through an accident which had broken two of its legs. This just shows how tough and determined hedgehogs are and that it's worth persevering with even the most traumatic injuries.

However, the big male hedgehog which was next into the chamber had a doubtful prognosis. He was not able to roll up and his two flaccid hind legs produced no nerve reaction when pinched with forceps. The X-ray confirmed that he had broken his spinal column with no chance of recovery and rather than let him drag himself into a prolonged painful death we decided to put him painlessly to sleep. Hedgehogs are such an awkward shape that the only way to guarantee a painless euthanasia is to anaesthetise them first. As this hedgehog was still in the halothane mask Russell could administer the fatal injection without any delay. Thankfully not all fractures of the vertebrae have this depressing outcome: some months ago we X-rayed a suspected paralysis to find that it had only displaced a vertebra, possibly leaving the spinal cord undamaged. After a few weeks of very, very close confinement the hedgehog regained the use of its legs and went on to be released, fully fit again. It's always worth a try.

These Bank Holiday patients began to look worse and worse. A female with infected fractures of both the tibia and femur of one leg was barely alive. I had already given her subcutaneous fluids and started the antibiotics but the leg was beyond salvation. Russell had no alternative other than to amputate it.

We had carried out amputations before but found that hedgehogs are very prone to post-operative shock after this operation. With an amputee we now continue the subcutaneous fluids for two or three days and generally give it extra warmth and an electrolyte replacement to drink. The operation had been carried out on an electrically heated pad, a procedure I would recommend with any small animal or bird which, because of its small body in relation to its skin area, can become hypothermic very quickly. When she came round from the anaesthetic I transferred her back to the box with a fresh hot water bottle to warm her for the journey back to St Tiggywinkles. She looked terrible but I was used to a hedgehog's resilience so had high hopes of her pulling through.

A badly infected crushed foot would need regular cleaning with Dermisol Multicleanse Solution, as would the hedgehog which had been scalped, a typical hedgehog injury. Surprisingly enough, there were no other head injuries that weekend; usually a fair proportion of our hedgehog casualties suffer from fractured skulls and jaws, as do the badger casualties.

Fortunately it seems to be the case that few hedge-

Often a simple plaster of Paris cast will immobilise a fracture until it heals.

hogs suffer from brain damage as a result of skull fractures. In the main the fractures are very far forward, usually involving the snout itself and the nasal passages. Without doubt, hedgehogs find this type of injury extremely painful and will often recoil and scream when the area is touched. There is no form of fixation available to assist the healing process, so once the damage has been assessed it is wise to leave it to heal by itself, hoping that breathing is not permanently impaired.

Hedgehogs appear very resistant to pain and seldom voice discomfort except, as in the case of snout injuries, if the pain is particularly severe. I am a great believer in the routine use of analgesics to ease the pain, particularly that which is borne silently by most animals after operations or treatment. The use of post-operative analgesics has been found greatly to assist the healing process: the beneficial effects, especially of the opiates, are thought to outweigh any unwanted side effects. Morphine and pethidine, however, wear off after a few hours and can seriously depress the respiration, particularly crucial when dealing with snout injuries. But buprenorphine given subcutaneously provides effective analgesia for up to 12 hours and appears to possess no damaging side effects.

As we saw earlier with Earthquake, fractures where the lower jaw hinges on the upper skull are as yet untreatable but breaks further forward and in particular across the symphysis at the front end of the jaw can be pulled and held together with stainless steel suture wire.

It's always the same with hedgehog treatment: so little has been tried and only now are the British public beginning to realise that some vets are willing to look at casualties. But many of these are working with treatments established for domestic animals and not designed to a hedgehog's special requirements. Many are eager for good information about hedgehogs, and I know that we would welcome any information whatsoever, which might help somebody somewhere save a hedgehog.

The types of injury likely to be encountered in a wild hedgehog could rarely occur in a dog or cat which is usually taken to the vet's at the first sign of a cut or limp. Because of their lifestyle, rooting around in soil and under leaf litter, hedgehogs usually manage to contaminate any open wounds before they are found and brought in for treatment. A hedgehog's wounds are nearly always purulent, contaminated and evil smelling, conditions seldom seen in small domestic animals. We at St Tiggywinkles together with Russell Kilshaw, our consultant veterinary surgeon, are willing to take in and care for any hedgehog, no matter what its condition. The only drawbacks are purely geographical, the distance between the casualty and us.

British Rail have agreed to carry hedgehogs from any of their parcel stations to Aylesbury station within 24 hours. However, they are aware of the Transit of Animals Order, which prohibits the transit of any animal if it might cause *unnecessary* suffering. Obviously this order was designed to protect farm animals; in fact, to follow the letter of its law would mean that the general public, veterinary surgeons and animal welfare groups would be contravening it merely by carrying an unfit animal to a place of treatment. Possibly any such suffering could be construed as *necessary* to save the animal's life.

As it is, there is sound evidence to show that hedgehogs have such good in-built shock absorbers in their spines that they would not suffer either necessarily or unnecessarily if they were carried by

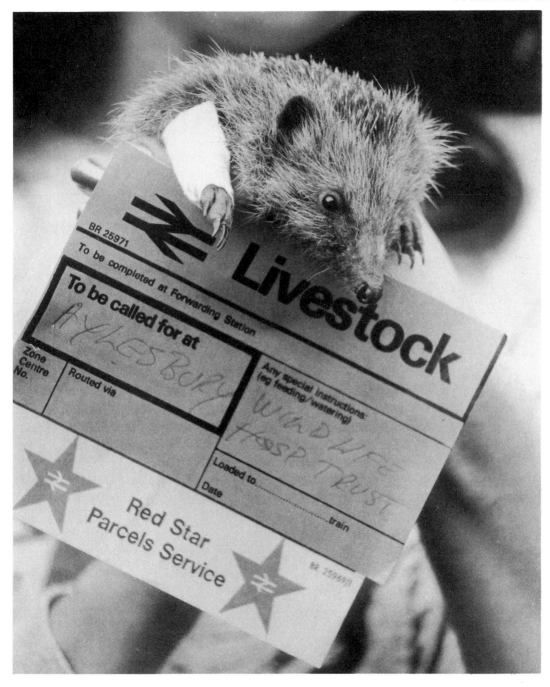

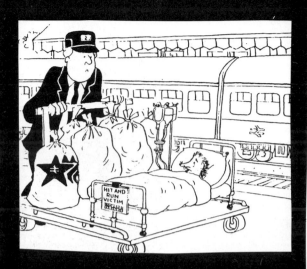

Rail mercy line for hedgehogs

By ALISON BATE

IT MAY be enough to make your skin prickle . . . but the kind-hearted British public is being asked to help save the hedgehog.

Wildlife lovers Les and Sue Stocker are coming to the rescue of injured hedgehogs by setting up a lifeline service covering the whole of the country.

And British Rail have guaranteed to deliver the prickly creatures to the Stockers' clinic in Pemberton Close, Aylesbury, within 24 hours.

They will be treated there before being released, fully fit, into the Buckinghamshire countryside.

Les, 39, and Sue, 35, formed the Wildlife Hospitals Trust seven years ago. They launched the Hedgehog Express venture because of the plight of hedgehogs during this summer's drought.

"The hedgehogs had trouble finding food and were run over in the roads in vast numbers," Les explained last night.

British Rail will charge a standard £5·50, plus VAT, for carrying the hedgehogs. They should be packed in two-gallon buckets lined with hay, with holes punched near the top.

"THANK YOU ST. TIGGWINKLE AND ★★★ !"

ST. TIGGWINKLE HEDGEHOG HOSPITAL

Hedgehog express

BRITISH Rail has agreed to transport injured hedgehogs by Red Star service from anywhere in England to an animal hospital at Aylesbury, Buckinghamshire, where vets at a new "St. Tiggywinkle's" unit there will treat them. Each delivery, costing the sender £5.50, is guaranteed within 24 hours, and plastic buckets are recommended as containers.

Bill Oddie's hedgehog sandwich.

train. Now all that British Rail require is a certificate from a veterinary surgeon stating that it is in the animal's interest for it to be carried to Aylesbury. Since people who pick up injured hedgehogs and send them by train have to pay the rail fare, it seems a shame that they might also have to find funds for a certificate. I hope it does not put them off rescuing injured hedgehogs – another worthwhile investment in the future of Britain's threatened hedgehog population.

It is said that a hedgehog's in-built shock absorbers are so effective that it could be sent through the post. One day the postman knocked on the door with a small parcel labelled 'Handle with Care, Hedgehog, it may bite'. In a panic I unravelled the parcel to find I was the victim of a typical prank by the actor and comedian Bill Oddie, one of the greatest supporters of St Tiggywinkles. Inside was not a real hedgehog but a 'hedgehog burger' made infamous by Rowan Atkinson and Mel Smith on 'Not the Nine O'Clock News'. I won't tell you what was in the *post mortem* report Russell sent back to Bill.

The Growing Race

IN SPITE of advanced veterinary techniques the hedgehog's small size still makes it impossible to establish for certain whether a female is pregnant or not. Our much publicised objection to the eviction of hedgehogs from North Ronaldsay was that even with a detailed examination, let alone the cursory glance the islanders were giving them, it was impossible to tell whether the female victims were pregnant, nursing with dependent families or somewhere between broods. Even the rather hazardous method suggested by one medical journal of palpating the abdomen of an anaesthetised female might detect unborn young only during the final days of a pregnancy and might cause unimaginable trauma to foetuses and a pregnant mother.

We learned early on in our work at St Tiggywinkles that there is always the risk that any female brought in might be pregnant or, even worse, might be the sole provider for a family of those tiny squealing babies which are helpless without their mother. Whenever possible any female casualty is released as soon as is feasible, as near as possible to the precise location where she was found.

One of our earliest encounters with the problem made us adopt a completely new procedure for those female hedgehogs which could not be released immediately. A female was brought in with netting wrapped around one of her legs. Even when anaesthetised so that we could dress the slight wounds there was no indication that she was pregnant. In fact she looked a little on the thin side. After a few days in intensive care her leg had healed sufficiently for her to join other convalescing hedgehogs in an outside pen. All went well until the second morning when, as I did my customary check of the nest boxes in her pen, I found the female frantically trying to protect a minute baby from the attention of her cannibalistic penmates. The baby was obviously newborn: the white spines had not yet broken through its skin and it blindly groped for the comfort of its mother's soft underfur.

Not wanting to leave my alien scent on either the mother or her baby I quickly, and painfully, gathered up the other adult hedgehogs and dumped them unceremoniously outside the pen door. They could be sorted out later but my main priority was to settle the mother and prevent further disturbance just in case she gave birth to other babies. However, I think she had no more after that. The other hedgehogs must have destroyed the rest of her family

A mother and baby must not be disturbed.

before I arrived on the scene and, although I took every precaution to safeguard that one remaining baby, the following morning the nest was empty. In her desperate anguish the mother had obviously eaten the sole survivor. Sometimes a disturbed hedgehog mother will carry her helpless youngsters to an alternative site but, unable to do this, it seems this hedgehog adopted the more drastic behaviour.

It's well known that the scent of humans on a litter of very young hedgehogs may make the mother desert or eat her young but this incident clearly demonstrated that any disturbance can have a devastating effect on a hedgehog family and even the sly peek into a nursery can be catastrophic. I often wonder about the effects on the hedgehog family of those 'outside the nest' photographs in magazines of mother hedgehogs and their newborn young. It's been said that after five days the young are safe from their mother, who will even adopt other young of a similar size to her own, but I will never take the chance of disturbing a nest and our only attempt at having an orphan fostered by a nursing mother at St Tiggywinkles was vehemently rejected.

The female hedgehog, locked in a pen, and struggling through the pangs of labour had seen her babies being taken one by one by the penmates. I wanted to comfort her, take her and release her in some generous wood full of tempting caterpillars and beetles, but she had to be kept in, at least for a few more days, until she had fully recovered from the leg wounds and that traumatic night. Still, nature takes its course and any female hedgehog which loses her young is soon back into oestrus, or on heat, and once again on the lookout for any passing male to sire her next brood.

Thankfully, female casualties are few and far be-

tween in the principal breeding months of May to July. Theirs is a restricted existence after they leave hibernation and are ready to breed at the end of March. They are noisily courted by the males who are spermatogenetic from April until August. Hedgehogs are thought to have a low fecundity but the frequency of sexual encounters, together with the hedgehog's exceptionally low mortality rate in the womb, ensures that over 50 per cent of the females will become and remain pregnant and will settle to build their football-sized nests ready for the arrival of their progeny. Meanwhile, males, who have nothing to do with domesticity, spend the whole of the summer roaming far and wide searching for food and receptive females which have already lost a brood or are late coming into oestrus. During the months from April to July we receive almost exclusively male casualties; the females, shackled by their responsibilities, do not roam far from their nests.

Even after July some females are found to be pregnant and may give birth as late as the second week in October. Nowadays any adult female we take in at any time of the year is kept isolated and weighed every day, although it's unlikely that one under 600 grams could be pregnant. During the last week of pregnancy the female puts on weight dramatically and for the two days before giving birth will be busy sorting out her bedding material, often cleansing an area right through down to the base of her pen. We tentatively inspect the pen every morning taking great care not to disturb the hedgehog in any way. Even if we cannot see any signs of new life we will not check the nest material until the female leaves to feed. We have had so many false alarms: I remember one female which we were convinced must be pregnant. After days of watching and wait-

ing it was proved yet again that you just cannot be sure.

Nobody can even be sure of the length of pregnancy in a hedgehog. Some give birth after about 30 days of gestation yet others seem to take anything up to 40 days. It could be that a cold spell of weather early in the pregnancy can cause the female hedgehog to resume temporary hibernation when her whole metabolism, including the development of the foetuses, would slow down. Very few young were born immediately after the extremely cold winter of 1963, most not until much later in the summer or autumn.

Once again legend has it that giving birth is so difficult for hedgehogs that they will prick themselves with their own spines to allay the pain. Of course this is not true and as the babies' spines are covered at birth with an insulating layer of oedematous skin, I don't think that giving birth is any more difficult than for most other mammals – provided that the births are normal, with the hedgehogs born head first and on their backs.

When the births are imminent the female stays in the nest, continually moving around as if in some discomfort. The babies are born with two rows of bumps along their backs where the spines are being held in. Even before the second baby is born, the first one's white flexible spines will have broken through the skin in two rows with a broad parting between the groups and none at all on the head. In Britain the average litter is four or five, whereas on the continent of Europe seven is a more usual number. Possibly feeding is better there, allowing the female hedgehog to take on more responsibilities, or perhaps the more extreme Continental weather conditions do not give the opportunity for a second brood. The desert hedgehogs, *Paraechinus*, have similar broods to the British hedgehogs, usually one to five babies, but the long-eared hedgehogs, *Hemiechinus*, regularly have larger litters though the babies are much smaller, weighing only 3 or 4 grams as compared with the European sizes of 12 to 24 grams.

The European hedgehog babies are tiny, only 50 to 75 millimetres long, with their eyes and ears closed, but by the time their 100 or so white spines are through they will have sensed one of their mother's ten teats and be suckling contentedly. Their growth is amazingly rapid. After only 36 hours the white spines have been joined by a set of darker spines, with the head gaining the first batch, and by 11 days they have mastered the supreme hedgehog trick of being able to roll up. They are now starting to look like hedgehogs: their bright button eyes open in the next couple of days, closely followed by their ears, and the coarse hair on their faces and stomachs starts to sprout when they are about two weeks old. By the 17th day they have a full set of brand new dark brown spines. They are now quite mobile, moving around the nest and constantly squealing for their mother if she is late for mealtimes. A young hedgehog's squeals sound more like a bird's than a mammal's, a very high pitched whistle that can be heard for some considerable distance. This is the distress call that has saved so many baby hedgehogs which have been lost or left destitute by their mother.

Before reaching the age of sight, hearing and awareness the baby hedgehog is quite helpless and reluctant to leave the security of the nest even if the mother, for some reason, should not return from one of her foraging trips. They may call out in hunger and cold but unless their nest site is within earshot of a Good Samaritan they will soon sink into hypothermic stupor and die. If they were a little older

Often we have to adopt youngsters only a few days old.

with their eyes just opened they would wander from the nest in search of their mother. It's these two-week-old waifs and strays which are often found crying so piteously as they wander through gardens and woodland, sitting ducks for any predator or blow fly.

These are genuine orphans which need rescuing if they are to have any chance of survival. Throughout the summer we take in many of these orphans and deal with hundreds of phone calls from all over Britain and Europe from concerned people who have found tiny whitish-brown hedgehogs wobbling around their gardens piping their distress in the vain hope of finding their mothers. The wobbling is a classic sign that they are cold, weak and have not eaten for some time. They will not be able to feed themselves for three or four weeks; normally they would not even have ventured out of the nest, under their mother's supervision, until they were three weeks old. If you're sure the mother is not going to

147

return, pick them up and adopt them: it's the only hope they have. Warm them up either on a hot water bottle covered with an old towel or in the airing cupboard; they will make no attempt to take any sustenance you may offer them until they are warm to the touch. However, before you do anything else, the orphans should be thoroughly checked for fly eggs or maggots. Do not worry about any fleas or ticks, these will not worry the hedgehog and can be dealt with when it is a little stronger. In fact to powder for fleas at this age could be very hazardous.

Before I go into the trials and tribulations of raising hedgehogs by hand, I ought to point out that sometimes even younger orphans and casualties may also need to be adopted. August and September appear to be the months when last year's autumn fall of leaves have composted nicely and are ready to be forked into the garden. I've already warned of the danger to wildlife of putting in the gardening fork without first turning the leaves gently. Often the mother hedgehog is accidentally killed while protecting her family or else flees the upheaval, never to return. All of a sudden you are left with a nestful of blind, deaf hedgehogs, some with their umbilical cords still attached, all needing at least four weeks' hand feeding until they may be able to feed themselves.

Sometimes of course the babies themselves are killed or damaged by the one fork thrust. Micropatches was brought in to us by a distraught gardener. The gardener had been moving his compost heap when inadvertently he had caught the newborn hedgehog with one tine of his fork. Luckily it had not penetrated the hedgehog; instead it had sliced down, between the two rows of white spines, opening up the skin in two enormous flaps. Naturally there was contamination of the wound but no bleeding

whatsoever, and after a good clean up with dilute Savlon, the two skin flaps were sutured together and Micropatches put reluctantly on a course of antibiotics. We are always reluctant to put very young animals on antibiotics as they may destroy the natural symbiotic gut flora that would just be starting to proliferate. As it was, we had no alternative and, rather than subject Micropatches to a course of injections, we gave him twice daily for five days the smallest drop of amoxycillin palatable formula designed to be given orally. He was then introduced to the nursery where he was given his own personal container.

There is a great worry, when taking in baby hedgehogs from various sources, that at any stage it is possible to introduce a virulent disease or germ. Just one baby with a salmonella infection can spread it to all the other youngsters in the nursery with often fatal results. By using mouse cages moulded in polypropylene we can isolate any solitary foundlings, often giving them a cuddly toy to curl up with, and keep small family groups separate from others. An overhead heat source, either a ceramic lamp or a tubular heater, will provide warmth at one end of quite a few cages, allowing the youngsters to move to the opposite end of the cage if they get too hot.

Strict hygiene is absolutely essential and wherever possible, by the time the hedgehogs are lapping, each container should have its own specific feed and drink dishes. Before it is weaned each hedgehog must have its own pipette feeder. After being washed, all the utensils, bowls, pipettes and containers are sterilised in Milton, just as they would be for human babies. Washing one's hands between handling each hedgehog is another way of preventing the spread of an introduced infection.

These young hedgehogs may have only their tem-

'You're throwing away all that's unique and precious in hedgehog culture.'

porary milk teeth and be quite incapable of feeding themselves. If they have been taken into care and are under twelve days old, with their eyes still closed, they will need feeding every two to three hours, with about 3 mls of a goat's milk/colostrum mix between the hours of 7 am and 11 pm. Newly born youngsters still with the remnants of their umbilical cords will also need two-hourly feeds during the night. Hedgehogs with their eyes just opened can take larger feeds, 5 mls, at longer intervals, three to four hours, and will not need feeding overnight as long as they have their last feed at 11 pm or later. At all times it is absolutely crucial that the hedgehogs are warm to the touch – being at room temperature or in a box near a radiator is *not* enough. If they become chilled, they will not feed, and will start on the downward spiral. However, it's surprising how little warmth will revive even the coldest of hedgehogs. A regularly changed hot water bottle covered with an old towel gives the direct heat that is so essential.

As you can see, adopting orphan hedgehogs is a commitment not to be taken lightly but, believe me, to watch a tiny waif obviously relishing a pipette of warm goat's milk makes the sleepless nights worthwhile.

We now have in care orphaned hedgehogs which will never again enjoy the benefits of suckling their mother's milk and colostrum, packed as these are with proteins and the immunoglobulins which help the youngsters build up immunity to infection. The hedgehog needs the colostrum for as long as 41 days, 2 weeks after it has started its first solid food. Without this prolonged period of taking in the immunoglobulins, young hedgehogs are highly susceptible to all kinds of infection, particularly to salmonella. This lack of protective immunity is probably the reason why most hedgehogs raised on powdered milk substitutes never make it to the weaning stage.

Obviously it is not possible to collect hedgehog colostrum to feed to the orphans but there is an alternative which is easy to keep frozen and, even more importantly, is readily available. Most goat breeders keep a frozen stock of goat's colostrum for hand-rearing neglected kids and, although it does not have all the same immunoglobulins as hedgehog colostrum, it offers good protection and has increased our hedgehog orphan survival rate to almost 100 per cent.

The goat's milk itself, mixed with the colostrum, is an ideal food for the raising of young animals. The fat globules it contains are smaller than those in cow's milk, making it much easier to digest. *Never give cow's milk to young hedgehogs:* apart from being pasteurised as most of it is, which destroys much of the goodness, it is quite indigestible for small animals and will lead to fatal enteritis and

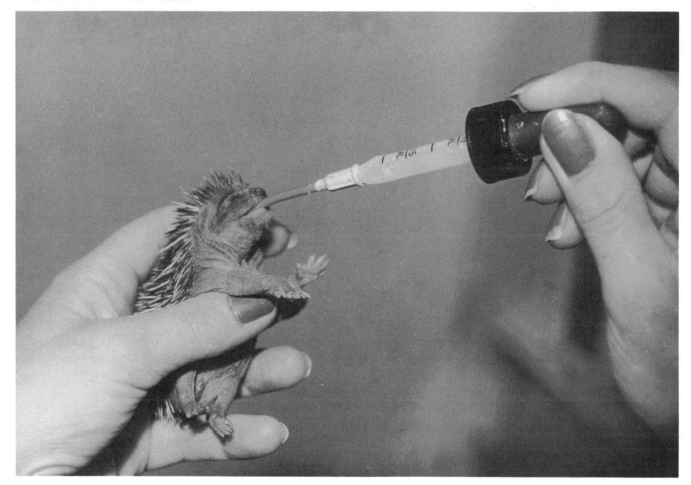

Feeding a baby hedgehog.

diarrhoea. Unpasteurised goat's milk retains much of the goodness so essential to a growing infant, but I must add a word of warning: it contains all manner of bacteria, both good and bad, so it is essential that it is offered fresh or freshly defrosted. Offering tainted milk can result in an explosion of unwelcome bacteria which can have disastrous effects for your charges.

Using goat's milk and colostrum, on the basis of two parts goat's milk to one part colostrum, has the advantage that ready mixed usable amounts can be kept frozen in small polystyrene cups sealed with cling film. When a cupful is used it must be *completely* defrosted, and each meal poured off and preferably warmed slightly before being offered to the animal. Failure to defrost it completely or even giving chilled milk can result in enteritis. Adding one drop of multivitamins, Abidec, to each defrosted cupful will make sure the hedgehog's progress is not impaired by deficiencies of some vital dietary constituents.

Should you be unable to obtain goat's milk colostrum, there is a substitute which can be made up. It may be better than no colostrum at all:

One raw egg (its albumen passes across the intestinal lining and into the blood, giving some protection against *Escherichia coli septicaemia*)
Half pint of water
One pint whole goat's milk
Half teaspoon castor oil (prevents constipation but cut down the amount if it causes diarrhoea)

Keep the mixture refrigerated, but renewed each day, and offer it as a temporary alternative to the goat's milk and colostrum mix.

The problem then becomes one of how to feed the tiny hedgehogs with the warmed milk mixture. Their mouths are small, far too small even for the kitten feeding bottles available from pet shops. We have had particular success using straight plastic droppers to which have been fitted 16 g hypodermic needles with the points cut off. Slid onto the end of each blunted needle is a short length of bicycle valve rubber with an overhang to serve as a teat (see p.150). As with all nursery utensils these should be kept sterilised: again, the Milton sold for sterilising human babies' bottles is ideal. To prevent any cross infection, it is advisable to keep a separate feeder for each individual baby and to transfer the cups of milk to small containers kept separate for each solitary hedgehog or family group. If you use cheap disposable paper or polystyrene cups and throw them away afterwards, there is no need for the constant washing and sterilising of durable receptacles.

Monitoring the weight of each hedgehog is an essential indication of its progress and gives early warning signs of anything going wrong. A simple weight record card for each animal, started the moment it arrives, will also be invaluable reference material for the following year when you will have forgotten all the trials and tribulations you met with this year's orphans.

After weighing the baby hedgehog and making the first record of its weight and estimated age, take the baby in one hand; holding it upwards and slightly forward with its back against your palm will allow it to 'paddle' its front legs over your thumb. 'Paddling' allows it to re-create the natural motion of pushing against its mother to facilitate the flow of milk from her teat. Taking the full pipette in the other hand, gently but firmly insert the soft part of the rubber nozzle between the hedgehog's tongue and the roof of its mouth. Slowly squeeze the bulb so that a little of the milk flows into its mouth. You can see at once if too much has been squeezed out because some of it will overflow from the side of its mouth: this should be avoided as the small creature will not be able to swallow the whole amount at one attempt and the excess can pass into its trachea and lungs causing inhalation pneumonia, the most common killer of baby animals artificially fed with a bottle or pipette. Proceed carefully at first: if you watch its throat you can see it swallow each mouthful. Both you and the hedgehog will soon get the hang of it.

At this point, after the first pipette is empty, it's important to try to simulate a hedgehog mother's natural action in stimulating the baby to empty its bladder and bowels. It is quite incapable of doing so on its own and this is one of the most important functions of a foster parent. We have had so many hand-reared baby animals brought in to our hospital dying because their bladders were bloated and their bowels blocked; yet the procedure of 'toiletting' is so simple. Holding the hedgehog in the feed position, gently but quickly, with the corner of a damp tissue or moist baby wipe, tickle over the hedgehog's anus and urinary opening with a back and forth action. The hedgehog seems to find great comfort in the essential practice and before long will stretch out its back legs and clear its bladder and possibly its bowels. At this stage do not be alarmed at the colour of its stools: they may be dark green but this is only where they are stained with bile because of its recent lack of nourishment. After a few feeds the colour should return to normal, which even then is a most peculiar shade of bright yellowish-green. Although there may be some evidence of excretion in a baby hedgehog's bedding area this is probably just an overflow, the red warning light that 'toiletting' is very urgent.

The colour of the stools is a good barometer of health in the baby hedgehog. Quite often there are tiny slivers of blood showing in them, a possible sign of coccidia infection. We have successfully conquered this even in three-day-old hedgehogs with a kaolin-sulphadimidine treatment given orally for five days. Before the hedgehog is on solid meat food the stools should be light in colour, of a putty-like consistency; if they become dark brown, there is some kind of enteritis present. The quandary then is that treatment should consist of 24 hours' starvation but this is likely to kill a baby hedgehog. To feed it on an electrolyte replacement, Lectade, is often the solution. Enteritis can be a prevalent killer causing dehydration and scouring so if you are in any doubt, contact your vet for a course of subcutaneous fluids.

After that initial toiletting, if all is well, continue with the milk feeding, giving altogether about 3 mls to a baby weighing 50 grams. Should the baby be reluctant to feed after a few mouthfuls, repeat the toiletting procedure as you should after any particularly large feed. Using the moist baby wipes sold for human babies clean any milk or dampness off the hedgehog when it has finished feeding and dry it with a tissue or piece of kitchen towel, paying particular attention to the area around the mouth and stomach. A few red sore patches may start to appear around the loins and tail area but a little petroleum jelly applied at each feed will keep these under control.

Put the babies back in their individual boxes on fresh paper towels, which should be white because the coloured ones may contain toxic dyes, with another paper towel to cover them to give the sense of security they seem to seek. If you should accidentally put two strange babies together, they will actively lick each other and then go into comical contortions trying to self-lather, a superb way of spreading nasty infection from one to the other. Keep them separate. They must also be kept warm at all times or the goodness they receive from the food will be used to keep them warm rather than in their development.

Go to any human post-natal clinic and see the different sizes of babies of the same age: some are big, some are small, some are massive and some are positively minute. It's exactly the same with hedgehog babies, so weights and sizes have little relationship to age or as a comparison with others, but they do serve to show the progress, or regression, of a particular individual. On average a young hedgehog will double its birth weight in the first 7 days of its life and by the time it is 6 weeks old it will have grown ten times as heavy as when it was

After feeding, it's essential to stimulate the baby hedgehog to empty its bladder and bowels.

born. Obviously some are going to vary from this norm but the increase shows that, properly fed, a young hedgehog should put on some weight every day. Weighing each baby at the same time each day does give an insight into its development but if one fails to grow as fast as another do not be tempted to overfeed it. Young hedgehogs live up to their names and will gorge themselves, given half the chance. As you feed them, watch that their tiny stomachs do not swell out of proportion to their size.

The weight records should show a gain every day although during the first few days of confinement there may be a slight loss due to the transition from their mother's milk to a substitute. After this first

Baby hedgehogs will start lapping goat's milk and colostrum after about 3 weeks.

levelling off, gradually add an extra pipette to each mealtime. It's surprising how soon you get the feel of each hedgehog and seem to know when it is not getting enough nourishment. A reason for not gaining weight could be that the baby animal is not being maintained at a warm enough temperature – about 25°C (77°F) is ample but remember to give the hedgehog an escape area in case it should get overheated.

As the hedgehog's first incisor teeth appear at about 3 weeks of age, offer it a low dish of the goat's milk/colostrum mix and gently push its nose into it. Once it gets the taste it will generally start to lick the milk off its nose and lips, gradually progressing to lapping from the dish. From now on, as well as continuing to pipette feed, leave a low dish of fresh goat's milk/colostrum in the box, away from the heater, so that the baby can take it as it wishes, but make sure it is changed and sterilised regularly. About this time you will notice that the hedgehog's weight starts to level off. After it has been two days at the same weight, mix some Pedigree Chum Puppy Food in with the milk dish. At this young age, it will not be able to digest adult dog or cat food. Also from now onwards make sure that the hedgehog is never without a low dish of fresh water.

Our procedure is gradually to separate the milk/meat mix until there are always three dishes on offer in the box: one containing Pedigree Chum Puppy Food liquidised with vitamins and dried insect food,

Young hedgehogs wean onto meat from about 3 weeks old.

another of fresh water and the third with the milk/colostrum mix. Watching the stools will show them changing to a well-formed brown, more like an adult hedgehog's. Eventually, at about six weeks, the milk mixture can be removed; but it can be reinstated if the hedgehog still has not been completely weaned on to the meat. It is necessary to judge their meat intake by their stools as the hedgehog habit of marching back and forth through their food makes it impossible to see whether it has in fact been eaten or, as is more likely, has been trampled into the floor of the box. This is the nearest we can get to a young hedgehog's natural wild existence where it and its siblings will go out foraging with their mother at about 3 weeks. It may chew likely looking morsels but will not start to swallow for another week, returning each time to the nest with its mother to suckle. Over the next two weeks it will gradually replace its diminishing milk intake with more solid food until it stops suckling altogether at between 42 and 44 days. To give our foundling a taste of a wild existence during the last two weeks before weaning we offer it a small dish of mealworms once a day. Too many can be harmful but a few add roughage to its intake of puppy food.

Mealworms can prove to be an expensive luxury but it is possible to start a breeding culture in a wooden box that can be kept in an out-of-the-way place in the garage or shed. Quite simply, fill the wooden box with alternate layers of newspaper and bran, add a few sliced potatoes and a few pieces of stale sliced bread and throw in two ounces of mealworms which are obtainable at most pet shops. Cover the top of the box with perforated zinc, because eventually the mealworms will metamorphose into beetles which can fly if not contained. Nothing else needs to be done except occasionally to add more sliced potato and bread. Do not remove the old sliced bread as this is where the beetles lay the eggs that become the next generation of mealworms. All this may take over a year to reach fruition but when it does so the culture becomes a continuous supply of mealworms with only the occasional topping up of the bread, potatoes and bran necessary to keep it active. In fact, no matter what age the hedgehogs they will appreciate some occasional mealworms and you will not have to pay the exorbitant prices charged in pet shops.

Between the age of 6 and 8 weeks the wild hedgehog teenager continues to go on foraging excursions with its mother. It now looks like a proper hedgehog; the third set of adult spines, which started to replace the first and second sets at about 17 days, is now complete. There are about 3000 spines at this age but as the hedgehog grows more will be added. Far more permanent than the first two sets, these spines last at least two or three years before being replaced one by one so that their loss is hardly noticeable. Its permanent teeth have almost replaced its infant milk teeth but the latter will not completely disappear for another eight weeks. Most of its brothers and sisters will have reached a similar stage of development which means they are ready to go out into the world, but approximately 20 per cent of hedgehogs born will never reach this stage of maturity.

Now their problems really start. It is known that 70 per cent of hedgehogs die in the first year of life,

with almost 50 per cent dying during their first winter. It's crucial that every hedgehog has enough weight to be able to survive the rigours of its first hibernation. Many that are born in second broods, late in the year, can never make the 600 grams bodyweight necessary for survival. Any orphans we raise are not thrown out just because they are 8 weeks of age and self-sufficient; we carry on feeding them until they weigh the magic 600 grams bodyweight and even then, if it is the middle of winter, we keep them till the following spring. Missing hibernation has no effect on the breeding potential of a hedgehog but keeping it in care over winter will make sure that it is able to mate in its first full year.

Young hedgehogs between 6 weeks, when they are weaned, and 8 weeks, when they finally leave the nest, have most of their problems ahead of them but if you are rearing hedgehog orphans your trouble will have started already. Apart from the problems of getting their diet and heating right, your young hedgehogs should now be so fit and strong that the neat polypropylene containers will no longer contain the adventurous little mountaineers. As fast as you retrieve one escapee from an inaccessible corner of your hedgehog house, another will have climbed out, tearing off in the opposite direction. Now is the time to consider building them much larger wooden pens which may also have to serve as their winter quarters. These pens should be large enough to allow the hedgehogs plenty of roaming space but compact enough to be kept inside for at least six months, a snug alternative to the perils of hibernation.

The two section hutches designed for rabbits offer

This young hedgehog has almost mastered the art of curling up.

ideal accommodation for one or two hedgehogs and may be easily constructed or bought quite cheaply at most pet shops. The closed nest area should be provided with a great heap of dried leaves, hay or newspaper – even the youngest hedgehog is quite capable of fashioning a comfortable nest that will keep it warm. One of the funniest sights every summer, at the hospital, is to see young, 2-week-old hedgehogs tearing and collecting in their mouths the white paper towels which have been laid so tidily at the bottom of their boxes. By the time they reach the age of 8 weeks they can build a substantial nest in no time at all.

The open side of the hutch, with the wire mesh, can be lined with a thick layer of leaf mould or fresh woodland soil. Regularly changed newspapers are a good clean alternative but do not satisfy the young hedgehog's urge to dig. Peat seems to be quite unsuitable. With a good covering in this open area most of the messy business of feeding and passing waste products will be done away from the nest area, allowing the sleeping hedgehogs to be virtually undisturbed. It is always a good idea to feel their stomachs as they sleep; a warm hedgehog is a healthy one, and any that feel cold to the touch should be taken out and kept under a ceramic heat lamp. Often just warming a young hedgehog will prompt it to resume normal feeding and drinking, but its stools should be examined for abnormalities. Probably after two weeks the hedgehog will seem strong enough to be able to return to the hutch but even then it should still be checked two or three times each day.

The time has now come, at 8 weeks old, to wean the young hedgehogs off the puppy food onto a more adult diet. We carried out a test with many of our rehabilitating hedgehogs and found that most of them preferred Co-op Supermeat liver flavour to the other brands of dog food offered. Once a week, sprinkle some multivitamin drops or powder on the food and offer a small dish of mealworms as a treat. However, it is important to ensure that all the hedgehogs have been weaned to Supermeat as some may be reluctant at first to leave the puppy food and will starve themselves rather than comply. A hedgehog which is not feeding has a baggy, empty feel to it whereas a happy, healthy hedgehog always has a full round stomach. Put the obstinate feeders back on puppy food, and then start the weaning process all over again until they comply.

The race to be fat enough to hibernate now begins in earnest: if these youngsters do not reach 600 grams in weight by November at the latest, they should not be allowed to hibernate. Keeping them instead in a temperature of at least 18°C (63°F) and feeding them regularly should keep them active until they attain that weight but even after that they should be kept warm, awake and well fed until the spring warmth of April and May allows them to be put outside ready for release when the last frosts are over.

Many animals which feed on invertebrate life rely on being able to find vast quantities of insects and other small creatures. The hedgehog has more bulk than most insectivores and consequently can find itself in trouble if the food is not available, especially during the colder months of the year when more food is needed to provide the calories to keep the body warm and mobile. It's a Catch 22 situation: just when the hedgehog needs more food there is less of it available. Either the insects and other cold-blooded invertebrates have died out or they have gone into hiding until the warmer weather returns in the spring. Even the earthworms which

When small hedgehogs are kept together, look out for bullies.

provide so much nourishment have gone deep into the soil where only the mole's deep tunnelling and the badger's tremendous digging powers can get at them. The badgers will remain sleeping in their setts if the weather gets too cold while the mole, unlike the hedgehog, has learned how to store a larder of paralysed earthworms just in case the ground becomes too hard to patrol. The other insectivore cousin, the shrew, needs to eat regularly but he is tiny and able to find enough small insects to keep him active throughout the winter.

It is therefore the hedgehogs and bats which cannot find enough food during the winter and have to resort to the perilous business of hibernation. Along with the dormice and the newly naturalised prairie dogs, these are the only British animals which adopt hibernation as a winter strategy. All the other animals, including the squirrels, seem to be able to eke an existence out of the meagre pickings of winter. Even snakes and lizards do not hibernate in the true sense of the word; they become inactive while hidden in a deep frost-free hibernaculum. The true miracle of hibernation brings about some very dramatic physiological changes which almost transform the warm-blooded hedgehog into a cold-blooded animal just for the duration of the coldest two or three months of the year.

Hedgehogs of the hot dry regions of the world, the desert hedgehogs and the four-toed hedgehogs, *Erinaceus albiventris*, aestivate during the driest part of the year. (Aestivation is similar to hibernation but in this case the animal assumes dormancy during extremely hot dry periods.) They do this by remaining cool, deep in their burrows, but if they are transported to a more hostile climate they quickly adopt the hibernation techniques of their more temperate cousins. Some desert hedgehogs were taken to Berlin in the summer and when left out in the open went into hibernation in temperatures of 19°C and even 23°C, which must have seemed cool to them. The tenrecs, which also aestivate in hot dry periods, will hibernate if the temperature drops below 10°C. The moon rats and hedgehogs of the humid tropical regions have no reason either to hibernate or to aestivate; in fact they meet no difference between seasons and will breed at all times of the year. No doubt if any were ever brought into more temperate climes they too would have the mechanism to induce the 'big sleep'.

However, 'sleep' is not really an apt description of hibernation or aestivation. In sleep all the bodily functions remain nearly normal, with the heart and respiration still continuing to keep the brain and other organs of the body unconsciously active. A hedgehog which is asleep can be seen dreaming and moving just like any other sleeping mammal but in hibernation its metabolism almost reaches a standstill. To all outward appearance it is dead; its feet, ears and skin feel cold to the touch but, as you touch it, unconscious reflexes make its spines stand up and tuck its head further into the impenetrable ball. Any sound will evoke the same response and yet the hedgehog's centre of nerve activity, the brain, is virtually closed down. Its heartbeat will have dropped from a frantic 190 a minute to a barely detectable 20 per minute. It hardly breathes at all, perhaps taking one breath every few minutes, and its body temperature, normally 35°C, drops to 10°C, a fall which would kill most other mammals. However, deep within the hedgehog ball the temperature around the heart is nearly normal, gradually lowering as you move outwards to the skin and appendages which are hardly warmer than the ambient temperature in the nest. Inside the hedgehog even more incredible events have occurred: 90 per cent of the hedgehog's white blood corpuscles have migrated to congregate around the stomach, intestines and bowel. These will fight any bacterial invaders from the remnants of decomposing food left in the digestive system at the onset of hibernation. The body does not want to excrete its precious moisture content during hibernation so small blood vessels around the kidneys will effectively have closed them down. The pancreas, the one vital organ which carries on functioning at full power during hibernation, maintains a constant flow of insulin to decrease the sugar levels in the blood to less than half the normal amount. As always, experiments have been carried out on hedgehogs, possibly with a view to applying their hibernation techniques to humans in order to further medical cryogenics and possibly enable space travellers to travel enormous distances while literally in a state of suspended animation. Insulin has been injected into hedgehogs and has induced hibernation, which could be maintained for two years, but although we know about the decrease in blood sugars there is still some query as to why a hedgehog doubles the amount of magnesium in its blood and how it reduces its body's oxygen requirement from 550 ml/kg/hour to 10 ml/kg/hour.

All told, the drop of around 25°C in a hibernating hedgehog's temperature enables the rate of chemical reactions in its body to be reduced by 75 per cent, allowing the fat reserves, that are its sole source of sustenance, to last much longer. Fat is automatically created when an animal eats more food than is necessary to maintain a healthy body. It is laid down in cells distended with one or several globules of fat which are then yielded up to the bloodstream in times of excessive activity, shortage of food, illness and during hibernation. Throughout the autumn

and early winter months a hedgehog builds up these fat reserves until they can be the equivalent of 30 per cent of its whole weight. Two types of fat are laid down, the white fat which collects under the skin and around the stomach and intestines, and the brown fat, known as the hibernating gland when it was first discovered, which is laid down around the shoulders, chest, neck and under the front legs.

The white fat is the slow-burn fuel which conserves energy and nourishes the recumbent hedgehog's slowed metabolism whereas the brown fat, which is in fact orange-coloured, is the supercharged fuel which boosts the hedgehog whenever it is needed. When a hedgehog is hibernating it is essential that its temperature does not fall below 1°C or it will suffer frostbite or may even freeze solid. It is obviously unaware of the outside temperature but if the weather turns very cold the brown fat is automatically brought into play: the quickly produced heat is then pumped through the bloodstream, warming the muscles, causing them to shiver and produce even more heat until after three or four hours the hedgehog's temperature will have risen by 25°C and its pulse rate to 320 beats per minute. It will then wake, realise that there is insufficient insulation in its present nest and move elsewhere to build another one.

Most mammals, including humans, have layers of brown fat when they are first born. Its ability to create heat twenty times faster than white fat is a safety valve to protect newborns after they leave the constant warmth of their mother's body. It is generally used up fairly quickly. Rats and mice always have a certain amount which is why they are able to live in cold stores and refrigerated buildings. In the hibernating hedgehog it is important to conserve these fat reserves because once they are burnt up there will be no food to replace them until the following summer. It appears to be more than just a combination of lowered temperature and shortened day length that brings on the drive to hibernate. Having sufficient fat reserves seems to have great bearing on a hedgehog's attitude which is why during the colder months the small hedgehogs try not to succumb to hibernation. Instead they are often seen wandering hopelessly in the vain search for enough food to sustain them. They realise they do not have the fat reserves to carry them through the winter and they go on searching aimlessly day and night until finally they collapse from cold and exhaustion into a deep comatose sleep; this is not hibernation, it's not even sleep. It is a downward spiral from which they will never waken unless they are rescued before it is too late. These are the autumn orphans which must be taken into care and fed all through the winter. Although the larger hedgehogs do not hibernate until very late in the year, these youngsters seem to know their fate as early as the first weeks of November.

It's not until November, December or January that the larger hedgehogs finally settle down to hibernation, when they must realise that the greatest threats they face are floods, the cold or predators which can destroy them while they are inactive. A great many will never survive until the spring, so it's as a last resort, when they just cannot stay out and about any longer, that they put the final touches to their hibernation nests. Last winter I saw hedgehogs out and about in the first weeks of January. There was still some food to be had: there are always a few slugs active and there is the carrion of other creatures which have succumbed to a sudden cold snap. In Britain the really hard frosts do not usually descend until the end of January with February and

MEMORIAL TO THE UNKNOWN HEDGEHOG

the first part of March being the time when any adult hedgehog out in the open is in trouble. The old story that hedgehogs start hibernating in October has now almost been dismissed, especially after a report that over forty recently killed hedgehogs had been found on seven miles of road in December when, according to the old writers, they should have been deep in hibernation.

During the months of November and December hedgehogs will be considering the safest places to build their winter nests. Under the roots of a tree, a bramble patch, down a rabbit hole or deserted badger sett, in a compost heap or even in a specially made hedgehog box: they like to find a secure place which will give them some protection from the worst of the winter weather. They love to build underneath timber buildings and sheds: in our rehabilitation pens they have the infuriating habit of digging down under the cosy nest boxes we have provided.

The nests they build may appear unkempt and ramshackle but in fact they are masterpieces of natural engineering which would put many birds to shame. Built of old leaves, grass and other plant material, the nests are sometimes 50 centimetres thick. Once the inside has been moulded into shape and all the leaves laid overlapping, the insulation can keep the temperature of the interior of the nest above freezing point, helping the hedgehog to conserve that precious fat-produced body warmth. So brilliantly constructed are these nests that once they are vacated they are often taken over by mice, shrews and voles which can enjoy the relative comfort and protection for many months.

Hedgehogs awaken fairly regularly during the hibernation period but seldom leave the nest unless the brown-fat thermostat has warned them that it is too cold, when they will not bother to add extra insulation but will go elsewhere to build a fresh nest. The resident hedgehog fleas seem to appreciate the warmth of a hedgehog nest and will stay on their host, tucked into the warmer underside of the curled hedgehog, whereas any ticks will spend the winter dormant in the lining of the nest itself.

Larger hedgehogs over 600 grams which have not yet been released should be kept in outside pens with weatherproofed boxes crammed full of dry hay and newspaper. Dog food and fresh water should be put out each evening, although if the weather turns very cold the hedgehog may go into hibernation.

In the spring, as the weather warms and their fat reserves run low, the hedgehogs start to wake from hibernation supposedly with a deep sonorous snore. The brown fat urges the muscles into action and raises the animal's temperature almost back to normal. The hedgehogs are very thirsty and have lost over one third of their bodyweight so they must eat if possible, just in case the weather turns cold again and they temporarily sink back into hibernation.

Once they have survived their first hibernation the hedgehogs' chances of survival are greatly improved for further winters. A one-year-old hedgehog can look forward to a much more secure future than it could before the previous winter – its first but perhaps the last for many of its brothers and sisters.

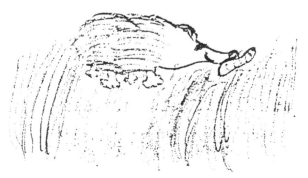

Katie Hooper

Not the End!

NOBODY REALLY knows how many hedgehogs manage to survive the rigours of each year's hibernation. In fact there has been so little work carried out on hedgehog census that not even renowned field zoologists will hazard a guess at the numbers remaining in Britain, let alone at the world populations of all the species of the *Erinaceidae*. From the correspondence received at St Tiggywinkles, I now believe that hedgehog numbers have been decreasing rapidly and that British hedgehogs in particular appear to have suffered more at the hands of civilisation than their cousins in less well developed countries.

Attempts have been made to calculate resident and migratory populations with a view to evaluating future hedgehog potential or decline but, as yet, the results have been so contradictory that we are no nearer solving the equation than when Zimmermann in the 1930s calculated the German hedgehog population at one for every twenty-five acres.

A clearer picture emerges in New Zealand where hedgehogs seem to be thriving in the milder climates. A census based on public observation showed that the hedgehog population there had rapidly increased up to 1948 and that it had remained stable until the survey in 1973. This may appear encouraging but perhaps a levelling off, in superb hedgehog country with little or no major predation, could in fact signify a reverse trend.

Probably because of its novelty as a naturalised animal the hedgehog is very popular in New Zealand and as well as the public surveys there has been a number of scientific projects to determine their role in and effect on the islands' ecology. One project on the natural wild diet showed an estimated population of hedgehogs on pastureland at between two and four per acre, yet near sand dunes, a habitat you would expect to be hostile, there were shown to be more than one per acre.

This kind of contradiction partly explains the extreme difficulty in monitoring a wild population of hedgehogs. It is such a resourceful animal that it will thrive on a variety of terrains but not at any regular density. In Britain Pat Morris studied the hedgehog residents of a typical West London golf course, ideal hedgehog country, and found one hedgehog for every three acres. However, another golf course elsewhere in the country might harbour more or less than this, and a featureless regulation Forestry Commission softwood plantation would

Inside St Tiggywinkles medical unit – the hedgehog in the incubator has just been brought in.

probably yield no hedgehogs, whereas in some conifer forests on the main continent of Europe hedgehogs have been known to make their nests of pine needles and to thrive on the invertebrates which have also adopted the acid environment.

There are good hedgehog areas and bad ones. The hedgehog of farmland and hedgerow is an animal of the past. Today's hedgehog makes the most of the

pedestrian-free linear habitat alongside busy roads or has moved into man's orbit, taking advantage of the relative security of gardens and finding superb trouble-free sites for nesting under outbuildings. It has been proved that beside the faster, busier motorways and dual carriageways, where they live with voles under fallen hub caps and feast on flies and other insects swatted to the sides by passing

Feeding time in St Tiggywinkles nursery.

cars, hedgehogs are safer than near other roads. Surprisingly, therefore, the continued expansion of the faster road networks offers some of the smaller mammals hope for the future.

Counting the corpses of hedgehog road casualties used to be the accepted method of assessing their numbers, but now populations are so small that you can drive for days without seeing any signs of habitation, and not because hedgehogs have evolved longer legs or learned to run from any approaching vehicle. I know of only one stretch of road where there are significant and regular numbers of corpses – a road which runs straight through Ministry of Defence property where modern farming practice has no place and wildlife obviously prospers.

At St Tiggywinkles we are determined to discover the state of the hedgehog population and to show that catastrophe can and must be avoided. We are now running a continuous hedgehog survey. All sightings, whether dead or alive, in the garden or on the road, injured or healthy, are fed into a computer so that eventually we should be able to establish the true situation.

*

When I gave up my business life to concentrate on freelance journalism, expecting to take in the occasional wildlife casualty, I imagined I would be ostracised as the nutcase at the corner of Pemberton Close. Little did I realise how many people felt as I did and desperately wanted someone to look after the injured creatures they found. The number of casualties grew to a torrent. What on earth had happened to them, I wondered, before we turned our back garden into a hospital? Sue and I could no longer support them on my meagre earnings as a freelance journalist with a growing overdraft, so the Wildlife Hospitals Trust was created and registered as a charity in order that donations and annual membership fees from animal lovers all over the world could pay for the upkeep of the hospital and help save the lives of wildlife casualties.

The number of hedgehogs in need of care ate deep into the hospital resources, and St Tiggywinkles was formed to concentrate on the many thousands of hedgehogs, often as many as ten a day, which flooded in from all over the country. As fast as we released twelve, another twelve arrived for treatment. I am sure we were keeping the dog food manufacturers in business. We needed more funds. Why not an adoption scheme like that at London Zoo? The only difference would be that after a few weeks our inmates would be returned to the wild. On the first day I took 508 photographs of hedgehogs for sponsorship and the British public responded magnificently, paying £10 for each hedgehog's stay in St Tiggywinkles. We were able to continue buying the best in dog food and now have the only veterinary surgery in Britain equipped with mini-instruments to cater for our tiny patients. People from more than fourteen countries have now sent their dollars, roubles, krone, francs and other currencies to St Tiggywinkles to adopt and support our hedgehogs, but most of all we must thank the people of Britain itself for making Aylesbury the hedgehog capital of the world.

It's not just the ardent conservationists who have made our work so gratifying. Hedgehogs seem at last to have captured the hearts and imaginations of thousands of people. Children have seen pictures and films of the animal world on television but the moment they visit St Tiggywinkles on an educational visit and see, touch and smell real live hedgehogs they become obsessed with their preservation: they write of hedgehogs, draw hedgehogs

St JohnsSchool
Walpole Road
Brighton
East Sussex.

Thursday   17th April   1986
Dear   mr   and   MrS   Stocker,
How   are   the   hedgehogs getting on?
HowNg are   all   the   other animals and the
owl   with   the   damaged eye? We are in
a   class   called Mi our School is
called? St Johns We would like to
sponser   a   hedgehog. We would like
to   help   a   hedgehog. from Jason Harris

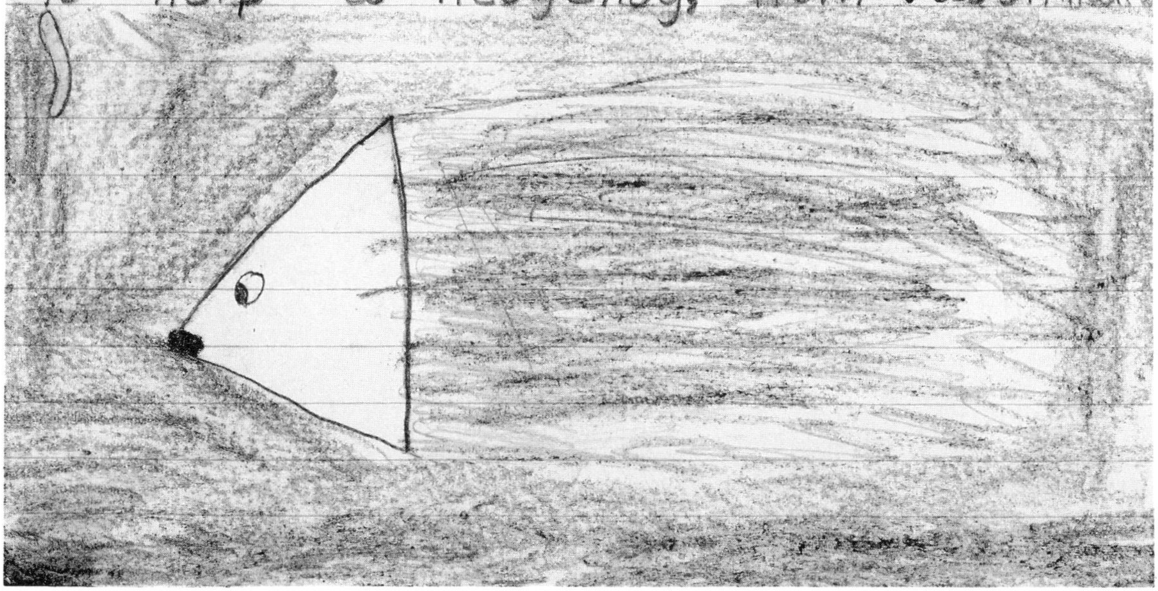

Sue holding Patches.

and constantly tell us about their neighbourhood 'pricklies'. Hearing these children we know that the long-term future for hedgehogs should be in safe hands, but in the meantime a great deal of work is still needed to ensure that the hedgehog population does not fall to danger level before it is too late.

All over the world people have responded to the needs of hedgehogs and their cousins in the animal world. There is now a World Conservation Strategy adopted by over thirty countries. Giant companies, the British Petroleum Company and British Telecom, have joined with smaller enterprises like Hedgehog Foods and Kiddicraft in supporting our project from its infancy.

As I walk through our intensive care unit and see those shiny black noses twitching to sniff my presence I realise that all those years on our own were worth it. These hedgehogs, young, old, fat and thin, can be released in the belief that if they run into further trouble there is a growing chance that someone will stop to pick them up. Their future is not yet bright, particularly in Britain where legislation on wildlife protection urgently needs reform, but it is definitely much rosier.

People everywhere are expressing their support for our work and slowly we are raising enough capital to build Europe's first purpose-built wildlife hospital. A great friend of wildlife, Mr Rob Clarke, of the Royco Corporation, has given the Trust freehold land on which to build the dream: we will be able to share what we have learned with others committed to the welfare of wild animals and birds, and in return will learn from their experience. Other people will be trained in hedgehog care and little rescue centres will be born all over the world from that one seed planted in Buckinghamshire ten years ago. And, once the caring but hoodwinked British public realises that bread and milk kill more hedgehogs even than does the motor car, our prickly friends can look forward to a secure future.

If you love hedgehogs, why not write in to us at **St Tiggywinkles, 1 Pemberton Close, Aylesbury, Bucks?** We would be happy to pass on all we have learned about hedgehogs and to hear about other experiences of these bold, endearing and useful creatures.

Now I must get on with my rounds: four injections to give, a dressing to change and there'll be the inevitable wrestle with Earthquake as he suffers the indignity of having baby powder sprinkled on his chapped stomach.

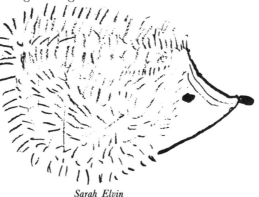

Sarah Elvin

The Wildlife Hospitals Trust

THE TRUST has been taking in sick or injured wild animals and birds for ten years and was accepted as a registered charity in early 1983. Through its fund-raising activities it offers help to any British wild animal or bird which is sick or injured.

Using all available veterinary and welfare skills its aims are to rescue, treat and then rehabilitate its patients to their wild state. Any animal or bird which can be saved but cannot be released is maintained in as natural a condition as possible for the rest of its natural life.

As part of its involvement in wildlife the Trust advises on all matters concerning wildlife welfare and publishes free literature on various pertinent wildlife topics.

St Tiggywinkles is the specialised hedgehog unit and hospital, and is a part of the Trust's general facilities at Aylesbury. It is wholly supported and managed by the Trust.

Apart from its obvious pioneering work with hedgehogs through St Tiggywinkles, the Trust is the only major independent unit catering for all British species of both bird and animal.

Supported by a thriving membership, which regularly receives its free news sheet *Bright Eyes* and other useful literature, the Trust is also pioneering through its projected hospital complex the teaching of both laymen and veterinarians on how to deal with wildlife casualties. If you'd like to help the Tenth Anniversary Appeal for Europe's first purpose-built wildlife teaching hospital, please send your donations to the address below.

With public support the Trust will be able to spread the facilities for wildlife welfare throughout Britain and into Europe, helping to save some of the millions of casualties that perish unattended.

If you are interested in the work of the Trust, send a stamped addressed envelope for an information pack to:

The Wildlife Hospitals Trust
Department CW
1 Pemberton Close
AYLESBURY, Bucks
England HP21 7NY
Telephone: 0296 29860

If you would like a detailed table of drugs and other agents useful in the treatment and care of hedgehogs, please write to or phone St Tiggywinkles at the above address.

Bibliography & Sources

I am indebted to articles by R. E. Brockie, J. Parkes and P. A. Campbell in the *New Zealand Veterinary Journal*, the *New Zealand Journal of Zoology*, *Nature* and the journal of the New Zealand Ecological Society for information about hedgehogs in New Zealand; and I have found the following books and papers invaluable:

Burton, M.   *A Zoo at Home* (1979) Dent
Burton, M.   *The Observer's Book of Wild Animals* (1971) Warne
Burton, M.   *The Hedgehog* (1969) Deutsch
Cooper, J. E.   'Anaesthesia of Exotic Animals' (1984)
            Animal Technology Vol. 35 No. 1 pp. 13–20
Corbet, G. B. & Southern, H. N.   *The Handbook of British Mammals*
            2nd Edn (1977) Blackwell
            Scientific
Dimelow, E. J.   'Observations on the feeding of the hedgehog'
            (1963)
Flecknell, P.   'The management of post-operative pain and distress
            in experimental animals' (1985) *Animal Technology*
            Vol. 36 No. 2 pp. 97–103
Gregory, M. V.   'Hedgehogs' *Manual of Exotic Pets* BSAVA
Harrison, D. L.   *Mammals of the Arabian Gulf* (1981) Allen & Unwin
Herter, K.   *Hedgehogs* (1965) Phoenix House
Hills, L. D.   'Pest Control Without Poisons' (1964)
            Henry Doubleday Research Association
Kingdon, J.   *East African Mammals* (1974) Academic

Macdonald, J.   *The Encyclopaedia of Mammals* (1984) Allen & Unwin
Majeed, S. K. & Cooper, J. E.   'Lesions associated with a capillaria
            infestation in the European
            Hedgehog' (1984)
            Journal of Comparative Pathology
            pp. 625–28
Martin, R. M.   *First Aid and Care of Wildlife* (1984) David & Charles
Morris, B.   The European Hedgehog (1967) UFAW Handbook,
            Livingstone
Morris, P. A.   'The Effects of Supplementary Feeding on
            Movements of Hedgehogs' (1985) *Mammal Review*
            Vol. 15 No. 1 pp. 23–32
Morris, P.   *Hedgehogs* (1983) Whittet
Orr, R. & Pope, J.   *Mammals of Britain and Europe* (1983) Pelham
Podushka, W. & C.   *Dearest Prickles* (1972) Spearman
Soil Association   'How Does Your Garden Grow' (1986)
            Soil Association
Soper, T.   Discovering Animals (1985) BBC
Stocker, L.   *We Save Wildlife* (1986) Whittet
Walker, P.   *Mammals of the World* (1964) Johns Hopkins
Wolf, E. & U.   *Der Igel unser nützlicher Gartenfreund* Hochrein
Wroot, A. J.   'Foraging in the European Hedgehog' (1985)
            Mammal Review March 1985 p. 2
Yalden, D. W.   'The Food of the Hedgehog in England' (1976)
            Acta Theriologica Vol. 21, 30 pp. 401–24

Index